Prescription Drug Addiction

The Hidden Epidemic

A Guide to

Coping and

Understanding

Rod Colvin

Addicus Books
Omaha, Nebraska

An Addicus Nonfiction Book

ISBN 1-886039-52-6

Cover design by Peri Poloni and Jack Kusler

This book is not intended as a substitute for a physician. Nor is it the author's intent to prescribe or give medical advice.

Library of Congress Cataloging-in-Publication Data

Colvin, Rod
   Prescription drug addiction : the hidden epidemic / Rod Colvin.
      p. cm.
"An Addicus Nonfiction Book."
Includes index.
   ISBN 1-886039-52-6 (alk. paper)
1. Medication abuse. 2. Drug abuse. I. Title.
   RM146.7 .C655 2002
   362.29'9—dc21   2001004894

Addicus Books, Inc.
P.O. Box 45327
Omaha, Nebraska 68145
Web site: http://www.AddicusBooks.com

Printed in the United States of America
10 9 8 7 6 5 4 3 2 1

To the memory
of my brother Randy

Contents

Acknowledgments

I would like to express my appreciation to the many people who shared their time and expertise so generously to help make this book possible. A note of special thanks to all those who shared their personal stories of recovery. Gary, Beth, Jeana, Margaret, Billy, Don, Justin, Terry, Caroline, Barbara, Jill, Devon, and Joni…your voices will resonate among those who still suffer.

The many others I wish to thank include:

Aristides Alevizatos, M.D.

Jeff Baldwin, Pharm. D.
University of Nebraska

Judy Ball
Drug Abuse Warning Network

Clifford Bernstein, M.D.
Waismann Institute

Sgt. Rod Bess
Virginia State Police

Milton Birnbaum, M.D.
Addictionologist

LeClair Bissel, M.D.
Addictionologist

Sheila Blume, M.D.
Addictionologist

Donna Brennan
Public Relations Counsel
to the Caron Foundation

Ray Bullman
National Council on Patient
Information and Education

John Burke, Vice President
National Association of Drug
Diversion Investigators

Phil Cogan

Carol Colleran, Director
Older Adult Services
Hanley-Hazelden Foundation

Bruce Cotter
Interventionist

Patrick Dalton
Addiction Institute

Robert L. DuPont, M.D.
Former Director
National Institute on Drug Abuse

John Fadie
NY Health Dept.

Betty, Ferrell, Ph.D.
Pain Researcher

David Gastfriend, M.D.
Addictionologist

Ronald Gershman, M.D.
Addictionologist

Terence Gorski
Relapse Prevention Expert

Sherry Green, Executive Director
National Alliance for Model State
Drug Laws

David Haddox, D.D.S, M.D.
Sr. Medical Director for Health
Policy
Purdue Pharma L.P.

David Hale, Agent
Oklahoma Bureau of Narcotics
and Dangerous Drugs

Sharon Hartman,
Program Director for Extended
Care Adult Services
Caron Foundation

Howard Heit, M.D.
Addiction / Pain Specialist

Sue Hendrickson
Caron Foundation

Tom Hinojosa
DEA Public Affairs

Alan Hollister, M.D.
University of Colorado

Gary Holt, Ph.D.
Pharmacist

Jeff Jay, President
Terry McGovern Foundation

David Joranson
Pain Research Group
University of Wisconsin

Ken Karp, Investigator
NY State Attorney General

Dr. Alan Kaye

Kathy Keough, Executive
Director
National Assoc. of State
Controlled
Substance Authorities

Keith MacDonald, Director
Nevada Board of Pharmacy

David Mee-Lee, M.D.
Addictionologist

Mike Moy, Chief
Drug Operations Section
Drug Enforcement
Administration

John Mudri, Retired
DEA Diversion Investigator

James Mulligan, M.D.
Caron Foundation

David Nielson

David Oslin, M.D.
Center of Studies on Addiction
University of Pennsylvania

Lt. Mark Petska
Virginia State Police

Russell K. Portnoy, M.D.
Pain Specialist

Barbara Roberts, Ph.D.
White House Office on National
Drug Control Policy

Kathleen E. Stinar
Hinsdale Newday Treatment
Center

Sidney Scholl, M.D.
Addictionologist

David Smith, M.D.
American Society of Addiction
Medicine

Paul Somsky, M.D.
Internist

Myron Weiner, M.D.
University of Texas
Southwestern
Medical Center

Susan Weinstein, Chief Counsel
National Assoc. of Drug Court
Professionals

Bonnie Wilford
Medical Education Consultant

Steffie Woolhandler, M.D.

Finally, I would like to thank Jack Kusler, Susan Adams, Rosalea Maher, Betty Wright, and David Zaloudek whose support helped make this book possible.

Introduction

If you or someone you love is struggling with addiction, it is my hope this book will offer you some insight about how to survive this turbulent time in your life. I certainly recall the chaos that addiction brought to my family. In fact, my researching and writing this book culminated as a result of my own family's tragedy with addiction.

October 19, 1988. My gift was wrapped and I had just picked up my blazer at the cleaners. The only thing left to do was decide on the right restaurant. The upcoming evening was to be one of celebration for my younger brother, Randy, and me. Not only had he just completed his college degree in business, but today Randy was turning 35. A birthday dinner was definitely in order.

But the birthday dinner would not come to pass. Around 3:00 that afternoon I got a telephone call at my office. It was a nurse from nearby Methodist Hospital: "Your brother has been brought in by a rescue squad…he's in critical condition."

Terrified, I jumped in the car and sped toward the hospital. "God, please don't take my brother," I prayed aloud as I raced down the main drag.

Minutes later, I was in the emergency room frantically scanning the bay of beds, but I could not find Randy. A nurse approached me and asked if I was Randy's brother. As she motioned me into the hall, I knew the worst had happened. "Is he dead?" I asked, not wanting to hear her response. The nurse dropped her gaze and nodded. Randy was dead.

The death of my brother—and only sibling—was one of the most profound losses of my life, but his early passing was not completely unexpected. For years, Randy had battled a prescription drug dependency that started at age 20 when his psychiatrist first prescribed tranquilizers to help him cope with anxiety. The drugs made him feel good, so he started relying on them and escalating the doses. Throughout the years, he obtained such drugs as Percodan, Percocet, and Valium by a common scam known as "doctor shopping"—visiting multiple physicians and feigning any number of aches and pains.

For years, my parents and I had long feared the toll his drug abuse was taking. We had encouraged Randy to get help—even offered to pay for treatment—but he always denied that he had a problem. Not realizing addiction is a progressive disease, we kept hoping the situation would improve. But it got worse.

Later, as I pieced together the last hours of his life, I learned that indeed prescription drugs—this time mixed with alcohol, a dangerous combination—had contributed to Randy's death. He had not overdosed, but years of abuse had weakened his heart. Finally, his heart had stopped—he died while taking a nap. My brother's long battle, our family's agonizing battle, with prescription drug dependency was over. Sadly, we had lost.

Randy represents just one of the untold numbers of individuals who get hooked on prescription drugs. This hidden epidemic continues to claim victims from all walks of life—executives, homemakers, health-care providers, and celebrities. They and their families are locked in the battle against prescription drugs. And, embarrassed by the "family secret," they suffer in silence and in shame. This serious national drug problem continues, misunderstood and underreported.

Still, there is hope for you. In fact, hope abounds. You need not live life battered by addiction. Treatment and recovery are absolutely real possibilities for all those who suffer. A richer, fuller life is within your grasp. Just take that first step—reach out. Ask for help. Trust me, there are people all around you waiting for you to ask.

Part I

Coping with Addiction

Although the world is full of suffering,
it is full also of overcoming it.

—Helen Keller
1880-1968

1

Understanding Addiction

Somewhere at this very moment, a man's wife agonizes as she receives a call from police—her husband has been arrested for forging prescriptions for tranquilizers. In another community, a mother weeps as her adult daughter, intoxicated on painkillers, is disrupting yet another family gathering. And somewhere within the walls of a respected hospital, a nurse is injecting herself with Demerol, a pain medication; her patient unknowingly gets an injection of saline solution. The case scenarios go on and on. Legions of Americans are abusing and becoming addicted to prescription drugs.

In fact, chances are you know someone who is abusing pharmaceuticals. Maybe it's your spouse, a relative, a friend, or a casual acquaintance. Maybe it's you. It's possible that you don't even realize the use has shifted from drug misuse and abuse to actual addiction.

Drug Misuse

Drug misuse refers to people who unintentionally use drugs improperly, hoping to get a therapeutic benefit from the drugs. Misuse includes many scenarios, ranging from the patient who stops taking a medication on his or her own to the patient who may be exchanging drugs with family members or friends.

If you're taking a prescription drug now, chances are one in two that you're taking it incorrectly. According to the National Council on Patient Information and Education, more than 50 percent of all prescriptions are used incorrectly. Misuse or noncompliance is a major health problem in the United States, resulting in 218,000 deaths and the hospitalization of 1 million individuals annually. The total cost to the economy is approximately $177 billion annually.

Another potentially fatal misuse of drugs involves painkillers or sedatives taken in combination with alcohol. Even though a drinker may have developed a tolerance to the sedative effects of alcohol, he or she will not have developed a tolerance for the alcohol's depressing effects on the respiratory system. The combination of alcohol and tranquilizers or sedatives can create cardiorespiratory depression and lead to death.

Drug Abuse

In *The Pharmacological Basis of Therapeutics,* Jerome Jaffe defines *drug abuse* as "the use, usually by self-administration, of any drug in a manner that deviates from the approved medical use or social patterns within a given culture. The term conveys the notion of social disapproval, and it is not necessarily descriptive of any particular pattern of drug use or its potential adverse consequences." Drug abuse may include using a medication "recreationally," using it for reasons other than those intended, or using the drug more frequently than indicated by the prescriber. Abuse may or may not involve addiction.

It is estimated that as much as 28 percent of all prescribed controlled substances are abused. That estimate translates to tens of millions of drug doses being diverted annually for the purpose of abuse. Diversion refers to the redirecting of drugs from legitimate use into illicit channels. The drugs may be obtained through any number of sources—by bogus prescriptions, from a friend, or purchased on the streets.

Drug Addiction

Addiction is a pattern of compulsive drug use characterized by a continued craving for drugs and the need to use these drugs for psychological effects or mood alterations. Many abusers find that they need to use drugs to feel "normal." The user exhibits drug-seeking behavior and is often preoccupied with using and obtaining the drugs of choice. These substances may be obtained through legal or illegal channels.

The American Society of Addiction Medicine considers addiction "a disease process characterized by the continued use of a specific psychoactive substance despite physical, psychological or social harm." Addiction is a chronic disease that is progressive—it worsens over time. It can be diagnosed and treated, but without treatment it is often fatal.

> *With addiction, there is a "resetting" of the body, a neuro-adaptation in the brain. One becomes dependent on the drug and tolerance builds.*
>
> Alan Kaye, M.D.
> Texas Tech Medical Center

How Addiction Affects the Brain

It was once thought that addiction was a result of being weak-willed—addicts could stop using drugs if they *wanted* to. But research has shown that this is not the case. In fact, after prolonged use of an addictive substance, the "circuits" in the brain virtually become "rewired."

When a chemical enters the brain, it is absorbed through receptor sites. Drugs of abuse entering these receptors are believed to act on the brain like the body's natural chemicals (such as *dopamine* and *endorphins*) that are involved in producing the sensation of pleasure. When the body is getting such chemicals from an outside source, the brain stops making some of its own and becomes dependent on the outside source. As the brain adapts to the drug's presence, the individual using the drug builds tolerance and must continually increase the dosage in order to achieve the initial pleasure sensations. However, most addicts in recovery report that they rarely achieved that initial sense of euphoria or well-being again.

Further, if the drug is stopped abruptly, it usually triggers a *withdrawal syndrome.* Symptoms may vary depending on the length of the addiction, but common symptoms may include anxiety, irritability, chills alternating with hot flashes, salivation, nausea, abdominal cramps, or even death. As one goes into withdrawal, the body "begs" for more of the addictive drug in order to escape the misery of withdrawal. Understandably, giving up the drug is difficult.

This inability to stop using the drug is a characteristic of addiction. Although an addicted individual may intellectually understand the destructive consequences of addiction, he or she may not be able to stop the compulsive use of a drug; the changes in brain structure can affect emotions and motivation, both of which affect behavior.

Another characteristic of addiction, *denial*, makes it even more difficult for the addicted individual to give up a drug. Denial refers to the addict's belief that he or she really does not have a drug problem. This self-protective mechanism keeps the addict from acknowledging both the drug problem and the underlying emotional issues that may be influencing the use of drugs. Usually, the longer the drug abuse has gone on, the stronger the denial.

How Many Are Abusing Drugs?

It's difficult to say with precision just how many Americans are abusing prescription drugs, although estimates are available. According to the National Household Survey on Drug Abuse, nearly 9.3 million Americans reported having used prescription drugs—stimulants, sedatives, tranquilizers, or pain relievers—for nonmedical purposes during the year 1999.

Type of Drug	Number Reporting Abuse
• Stimulants	2,302,000
• Pain Relievers	6,634,000
• Tranquilizers	2,793,000
• Sedatives	632,000

To enhance the accuracy of the household data, the survey is conducted in person and interviewees are allowed to self-administer the questions on drug abuse. However, those who administer the survey consider the results "conservative," and many experts consider the projections low, citing the probability that some respondents were not honest.

Still, additional data suggests the magnitude of the problem. Statistics from the Substance Abuse and Mental Health Services Administration show that 30 to 50 percent of those drugs listed by patients treated for misuse or overdose in hospital emergency rooms are prescription drugs. It's important to note, however, that the emergency room data likely inflate abuse statistics since suicide attempts are included.

According to other estimates, between 10 and 16 percent Americans are identified as being chemically dependent at some point in life. These percentages refer to alcohol addiction as well. However, many individuals in recovery report that they often used both alcohol and prescription drugs, depending on their availability. A 1998 report by the University of Chicago states that multi-drug consumption is the normal pattern among a broad range of substance abusers.

Symptoms of Addiction

Prescription drug abuse is often difficult for friends and family to recognize. Contrary to popular belief, one need not abuse drugs daily to have a problem with addiction; the pattern of abuse may be occasional or habitual. The abuse is usually an intensely private affair between the abuser and a bottle of pills. And, the pilltaker is not subject to the social stigma associated with the shadowy world of street drug dealing. Still, the following are symptoms of addiction:

- Showing relief from anxiety
- Changes in mood—from a sense of well-being to belligerence
- False feelings of self-confidence
- Increased sensitivity to sights and sounds, including hallucinations

- Altered activity levels—such as sleeping for 12 to 14 hours or frenzied activity lasting for hours
- Unpleasant or painful symptoms when the substance is withdrawn
- Preoccupation with running out of pills

Distinguishing Medical Substance Use from Nonmedical Substance Use

	Medical Use	**Nonmedical Use**
Intent	To treat diagnosed illness	To alter mood
Effect	Makes life of user better	Makes life of user worse
Pattern	Steady and sensible	Chaotic and high dose
Legality	Legal	Illegal (except alcohol or tobacco use by adults)
Control	Shared with physician	Self-controlled

From "Benzodiazepines, Addiction and Public Policy" by Robert L. DuPont, M.D., New Jersey Medicine, 90 (1993): 824-826. Reprinted by permission.

Risks for Addiction

Who is at risk for addiction? The risk for addiction is greatest among women, seniors, and adolescents. Women are two to three times more likely than men to be prescribed drugs such as sedatives; they are also about two times more likely to become addicted. This stems in large part from the fact that women are more likely to seek medical attention for emotional problems. Seniors take more drugs than the rest of the population, increasing their odds of becoming addicted. Finally, 1999 national studies show that the sharpest increase of users of prescription drugs for nonmedical purposes occurs in the 12 to 17 and 18 to 25 age groups.

The following are also considered risk factors for addiction:
- Medical condition that requires pain medication
- Family history of addiction
- Excessive alcohol consumption
- Fatigue or overwork
- Poverty
- Depression, dependency
- Poor self-concept, obesity

Other groups at increased risk for addiction are medical professionals, drug abusers, former addicts, alcoholics, and smokers. Additionally, extreme stress such as family tragedy, death, or divorce may precipitate abusive drug use.

Is anyone who takes addictive drugs at risk for addiction? The answer is no. "Fifteen years ago, it was widely believed that virtually anyone who took psychoactive drugs was a likely candidate for dependency, but that thinking has changed," according to Bonnie Wilford, medical education consultant with the Center for Health and Services Outcomes Research in Washington, D.C. "Our change of thought has come about as a result of our increased knowledge about addiction. For example, perhaps seven out of ten people could take tranquilizers and not progress to addiction. But those who do become addicted likely have a pre-existing addictive disorder, such as predisposition to alcoholism. The difficulty is, we don't always know which patients this will be."

The "Unwitting" Addict

Many individuals who become dependent on prescription drugs are referred to as "unwitting" addicts. You, a friend, or a loved one may be among this group. Initially, many of these individuals did not realize the drug they were taking had addiction potential. But, whether or not they knew, these individuals had no history of drug abuse or addiction. Rather, they first started using a prescribed drug for a legitimate medical problem, physical or emotional. For example, it may have been a painkiller for a back injury or a sedative for anxiety. Then, at some point, they started increasing the dosages on their own because the drug made them feel better—relief from physical or emotional distress. The nature of the drug required that they continue escalating the dosages to get the desired effect. Gradually, the abuse became full-blown addiction.

Physiological Dependence vs. Addiction

Not all drug dependence is addiction. *Physiological dependence,* which is often confused with addiction, is a result of the body's adaptation to a drug used over a period of time to treat a medical disorder. For example, a patient taking pain medication for several weeks would likely develop some degree of tolerance to the drug; he or she would become physically dependent, and would have withdrawal symptoms if the drug were stopped abruptly. This type of dependence, however, is *not* addiction. A patient with a physiological dependence can quit the drug, usually by being tapered off it gradually, with medical supervision and without admission into a drug treatment program.

Distinction Between Addiction and Physiological Dependence

Addiction

- Loss of control
- Continued use despite problems caused by use
- Denial
- Relapse
- A complex, biobehavioral, lifelong, malignant problem
- Limited to chemically dependent people
- Not a complication of medical treatment unless a prior history of chemical dependence exists
- Best treated by specific chemical dependence treatment

Physiological dependence

- A cellular adaptation to the presence of a substance
- Withdrawal symptoms on abrupt discontinuation
- Not associated with relapse
- A benign, temporary problem
- Common to many substances used in medicine including steroids, antidepressants, anti-epilepsy, and antihypertensive medicines
- Best treated by gradual dose reduction

Which Drugs Are Being Abused?

According to the Drug Abuse Warning Network (DAWN), fourteen of the top twenty most abused mood-altering substances in the United States are prescription drugs. Benzodiazepines, which are sedatives, rank highest on the list, followed by the opioids or painkillers. This list of drugs is gathered during hospital emergency room visits across the nation. To be classified as an abuse episode, the patient must indicate that a drug was being used for purposes of recreation or dependence.

Top 20 Most Abused Mood-Altering Substances in the U.S.

1.	Alcohol-in-combination	12.	Methamphetamine *(Desoxyn, speed)*
2.	Cocaine	13.	Trazodone *(Desyrel)*
3.	Marijuana	14.	Carisoprodol *(Soma)*
4.	Heroin/morphine	15.	Oxycodone *(OxyContin, Percocet, Percodan, Tylox)*
5.	Unspecified benzodiazepine		
6.	Alprazolam *(Xanax)*	16.	Valproic acid *(Depakote)*
7.	Clonazepam *(Klonopin)*	17.	Propoxyphene *(Darvocet N, Darvon)*
8.	Hydrocodone *(Vicodin, Lorcet, Lortab)*		
9.	Amphetamine *(Dexedrine)*	18.	Amitriptyline *(Elavil)*
10.	Diazepam *(Valium)*	19.	Methadone
11.	Lorazepam *(Ativan)*	20.	LSD

From Drug Abuse Warning Network Emergency Room Data. Based on drugs mentioned during emergency room visits in 2000.

Commonly Abused Prescription Drugs by Class

Opioids

Opioids, also known as *opiates*, are typically prescribed to relieve acute or chronic pain such as that from cancer or surgery. This class of drugs is also referred to as *narcotic analgesics* or pain relievers. For acute pain, opioids are normally used only for short periods—less than 30 days. Opioids may be taken orally or by injection.

Although they are medically indicated for the control of pain, opioids are drugs with high abuse potential. In addition to blocking pain messages being sent to the brain, opioids produce feelings of euphoria or pleasure. It is this sensation that makes the drug highly sought after by those wishing to free themselves from painful emotions. Chronic use of opioids results in both tolerance and dependence.

Opioid Abuse

The abuse of opioids has been an ongoing problem since the 1960s; however, statistics based on hospital emergency room visits show that in 1996 the incidence of opioid abuse doubled. Although the abuse has been recorded among all socioeconomic groups, it is sometimes referred to as a "white-collar addiction," given the numbers of professional people who abuse the drug.

Common opioid products include:

Darvocet	Methadone	Roxiprin
Darvon	Morphine	Tussionex
Demerol	OxyContin	Tylenol with Codeine
Dilaudid	Percocet	Vicodin
Lorcet	Percodan	
Lortab	Roxicet	

Opioid Withdrawal

Stopping the use of opioids suddenly will bring on symptoms of withdrawal. Initial withdrawal symptoms usually begin within hours of the last dose and may include: cravings, runny nose, excessive sweating, insomnia, and yawning. Those who have been addicted to opioids for a long time may progress to severe withdrawal symptoms, including: chills, fever, muscle spasms, abdominal pain, seizures, coma, and even death.

Cessation of opioids is best accomplished under medical supervision, where withdrawal can be managed. A medically assisted withdrawal is safer and also increases the chance that an individual will "come off" a drug.

Stimulants

Stimulants are drugs that stimulate the central nervous system, increasing mental alertness, decreasing fatigue, and producing a sense of well-being. These drugs are often prescribed for attention deficit disorder (hyperactivity) and narcolepsy, a condition characterized by falling asleep:

> Adderall
> Cylert
> Dexedrine
> Ritalin

Interestingly, while the drugs listed above stimulate the central nervous system in adults, they have a calming effect on children. Consequently, these stimulants are often prescribed for children diagnosed with attention deficit disorder (hyperactivity). In these children, the drugs produce a calming effect by stimulating nerves that slow down other overactive nerves.

In adults, other stimulants such as Fastin, Didrex, Meridia, Plegine, Sanorex, and Tenuate may be used to suppress appetite.

Stimulant Abuse

Stimulants such as Dexedrine and Ritalin increase the amount of the natural brain chemicals *norepinephrine* and *dopamine*. The increased levels of these chemicals create both an increased heart rate and blood pressure and a sense of pleasure, resulting in an overall sense of heightened energy and sense of well-being. Once accustomed to an outside source of these chemicals, the body craves more of them.

Anyone taking high doses of stimulants runs the risk of irregular heartbeat and high blood pressure, which can result in heart failure. High doses may also result in feelings of hostility and paranoia.

Stimulant Withdrawal

Symptoms of withdrawal from stimulants include: depression, fatigue, loss of interest or pleasure in daily activities, insomnia, loss of appetite, suicidal thoughts and behavior, and paranoid delusions.

Sedatives

Sedatives such as *benzodiazepines* depress the central nervous system and are frequently used to treat anxiety, panic disorder, or insomnia; some are also used for seizure disorders. As these drugs interact with chemicals in the brain, they cause a reduction in brain activity, and bring about the sedative effect. Benzodiazepines often prescribed for daytime use:

Ativan	Librium
Serax	Tranxene
Valium	Xanax

Benzodiazepines frequently used for nighttime insomnia:

Dalmane	Doral
Halcion	ProSom
Restoril	

Benzodiazepines used for seizure disorders:

Klonopin	Tranxene
Valium	

Benzodiazepine Abuse

Benzodiazepines are among the most abused prescription drugs in the nation. They were first introduced into American medicine in 1960 for anxiety. Today, it's estimated that between 10 and 12 percent of the population use benzodiazepines within the course of a year. According to the Drug Abuse Warning Network, most deaths from benzodiazepines are caused by combined use with alcohol.

Short-Term vs. Long-Term Use

Debate continues in the medical community over the safe, long-term use of benzodiazepines, since the buildup of tolerance is often rapid and severe withdrawal can occur if these drugs are stopped abruptly. Short-term use is considered a few weeks or less; long-term use refers to several months or more. The debate prompted the American Psychiatric Association to issue a statement claiming, "Physiological dependence on benzodiazepines...can develop with therapeutic doses. Duration of treatment determines the onset of dependence...clinically significant dependence usually does not appear before four months of such daily dosing. Dependence may develop sooner when higher, anti-panic doses are taken daily."

Benzodiazepine Withdrawal

Symptoms of withdrawal from benzodiazepines and other sedatives include: insomnia, anxiety, depression, euphoria, incoherent thoughts, hostility, grandiosity, disorientation, tactical/auditory/visual hallucinations, and suicidal thoughts. Symptoms can progress to include abdominal cramps, muscle cramps, nausea or vomiting, trembling, sweats, and seizures.

Anyone who has used benzodiazepines over an extended period of time—several weeks or more—should never stop taking the drug abruptly. After long-term use, medically unsupervised withdrawal can be severe, leading to delirium, fever, seizures, coma, and even death. Individuals wishing to stop the drug should ask their physicians about being medically supervised so that withdrawal can be managed as use of the drug is tapered.

Another symptom of withdrawal is "symptom rebound," an intensified return of the original symptoms (such as insomnia or anxiety) for which the drug was first prescribed. This rebound is often misinterpreted by patients as a recurrence of anxiety.

A Risk for Patients Prone to Addiction

Some of the controversy surrounding the use of benzodiazepines has resulted from the dependency problems occurring among patients who have had previous problems with addiction. "Patients who have a history of chemical dependence, including the use of alcohol or drugs, are poor candidates for use of benzodiazepines in the treatment of anxiety," states Robert L. DuPont, M.D., former director of the National Institute on Drug Abuse. "Anyone who has used illicit drugs repeatedly over a period of months or years, and anyone who drinks more than a few drinks of alcohol a week, should use benzodiazepines with extreme caution, if at all."

Benzodiazepine Checklist

Questions to consider for long-term benzodiazepine prescriptions:

1. **Diagnosis and response to treatment**
   Does the patient have a clear-cut diagnosis, and does the patient respond favorably to the use of the benzodiazepine?

2. **Use of psychotropic substances**
   Is the patient's use of alcohol and other substances legal and sensible? Does the patient avoid all use of illegal drugs?
   Is the benzodiazepine dose reasonable? Is the use of other prescribed drugs medically reasonable?

3. **Toxic behavior**
   Is the patient free of slurred speech, accidents, or other problems that may be associated with excessive or inappropriate use of any prescribed or nonprescribed psychoactive substance?

4. **Family monitor**
   Does a family member confirm that the patient's use of the benzodiazepine is both sensible and helpful and that the patient does not abuse alcohol or use illegal substances?

A "no" answer to any of these questions suggests the need to discontinue benzodiazepines. A "yes" to all four questions supports continuation of benzodiazepine prescriptions if that is the shared conclusion of the patient and the physician. The standard to be met: Is this treatment clearly in the patient's best interest?

From "Benzodiazepines, Addiction and Public Policy," by Robert L. DuPont, M.D., *New Jersey Medicine* 90 (1993): 824-826. Reprinted by permission.

Prescription Drug Abuse Checklist

Ask yourself the following questions about opioids, sedatives, and stimulants:

☐ Have you been taking sleeping pills every day for more than three months?

☐ Do you sometimes take pills in order to make life more bearable?

☐ Have you tried to stop taking pills and felt vulnerable or frightened?

☐ Have you tried to stop taking pills and felt your body start to tremble or shake?

☐ Do you continue to take pills even though the medical reason for taking them is no longer present?

☐ Do you think pills are more important than family and friends?

☐ Are you mixing pills with wine, liquor, or beer?

☐ Are you taking one kind of pill to combat the effects of another pill?

☐ Do you take pills to get high and have fun?

☐ Do you take pills when you're upset or to combat loneliness?

☐ Do you feel happy if your doctor writes a prescription for drugs that change your mood?

☐ Do you visit several doctors to get the same prescription?

☐ Are you taking more pills to achieve the same effect you used to experience with smaller doses?

☐ Do you find it difficult to fulfill work obligations when you're taking pills?

☐ Do you ever promise yourself that you will stop taking pills, and then break the promise?

If you answer *yes* or *sometimes* to three or more of these questions, you may be developing a problem with drug dependence. Talk with a chemical dependency counselor or doctor who specializes in treating drug problems. For referral to a local resource, call 1-800-NCA-CALL (622-2255).

Reprinted with permission from the Women's Alcohol and Drug Education Project, Women's Action Alliance, Inc.

2

Voices of Recovery

Seven million Americans are in recovery from addictive diseases. In this chapter you'll hear the stories of several individuals recovering from addiction to prescription drugs. Some of them underwent serious ordeals that nearly cost them their lives. Their stories clearly demonstrate that addiction is a progressive disease.

In many of these stories, you'll note the individuals were "unwitting" addicts. They had not abused drugs previously, but began using the drugs for legitimate reasons. When the medications relieved emotional pain, the abuse began and they began their descent into addiction. As several individuals explain, they were slow to realize that their therapeutic use of medication had escalated to abuse.

Listen carefully to their voices. Their message is clear: Recovery is possible. A better, richer life is possible.

Gary, 40
Businessman

Looking back, I realize I am an alcoholic, but I had never let my drinking get out of control until 1999. I had begun drinking more then because I was under a lot of stress with my work—I owned several companies. I was also married and had three small children. Still, I managed to exercise rigorously; I'm a runner.

I started working out with a personal trainer at my gym. As we got to know each other, I told him that I was overextended and stressed a great deal of the time. He took me in his office and said, "I've got something that can help you." He handed me a pill. I asked him what it was and whether it had any side effects. I had never abused pills before. He told me it was just a pain pill, that he and his brother-in-law had taken them for a couple of years with no problem. So, I took one—20 milligrams, the size of an aspirin. The pill was OxyContin, which I had never heard of. It is a very strong pain medication that also has a very high potential for addiction. My descent into pure hell was about to begin.

In the beginning, the drug was absolutely wonderful. It was the answer to all my problems. I felt euphoric. I felt in control. And strangely, I felt organized. I could handle all my business and family matters. I could handle the world, I thought. I bought about 30 pills for about $10 a piece. They lasted about ten days. I was taking two or more pills a day.

Then I ran out of pills. I started feeling so bad, I couldn't get out of bed. I thought I had a severe case of the flu. My muscles ached. I didn't realize it at the time, that I was going through withdrawal. I talked to my trainer from the gym, who told me I was in withdrawal and that I needed more drugs. So, I bought some more—anything to get over feeling so sick. When I bought the second batch from him it was the first time I knew what they were called. He called them "Oxys." I realized that I was addicted already. I took a pill and felt better almost immediately. My wife thought I had a 24-hour flu.

Three months later, I was still taking the Oxys. But I was training for a marathon, a 26-mile race, and I was having trouble—my muscles kept aching. So, I took more pills. Although I wasn't feeling euphoric anymore, like I did in the beginning, I was having to take the pills just to keep from getting sick. My tolerance went through the roof so quickly. By now, I was taking about 20 pills a day. I was still seeking the "buzz" I had gotten the first time I took them. I had learned I could get a faster "fix" by chewing the pills or crushing them and then snorting them.

The day of the marathon, I had pills in my running shorts. I knew I would need them. But 13 miles into the race, I could not make it. I walked and shuffled through the last 13 miles. Once I got into the runners' tent, I was a mess. Everyone thought I was having heat exhaustion. In reality, I was needing more drugs, even though I had taken 40 that day.

About a month later, I was such a mess, I finally told my wife that I was addicted to OxyContin. She called the police and reported the trainer. It turns out he was a dealer who had gotten four other people addicted. He was getting the drug from a crooked doctor, who was arrested and barred from practicing.

My wife was supportive and I decided to go into treatment. I went into a rehab hospital, where I was undergoing detox, but I stayed only eight days. I didn't think I needed treatment, and I wanted to go on vacation with my family. But very soon I started feeling sick again. Not only my muscles ached, but it felt like even my bones ached. Amazingly, I stuck it out and in a few weeks was feeling better again. I stayed off OxyContin…for a while.

About a year later, I was under a great deal of pressure. I had made a huge business purchase and was a couple of million dollars in debt. Believe it or not, I called the guy who had gotten me hooked the first time. Within five minutes he was at my office with more OxyContin. I began using the drug again.

I really believed I could use the pills just a little, as I needed them. But within two weeks, I was back up to 20 pills a day, and they were costing me $20 a pill, twice the price I first paid. After several months, I broke down and told my wife I was using Oxys again.

I went into another treatment center, and they kept me for only three days (in detox), then told me to go home and continue as an outpatient. Within an hour of leaving the facility, I was going through withdrawal. I had the "skin crawls," which felt like bugs crawling all over me. Within two days, I was using Oxys again.

Sadly, over the next six months I got clean and then relapsed three times before I finally decided to get serious about treatment. Each time, all it took was one pill. One pill and I was a full-fledged addict. And each time, I would lie to my wife about using the drug. Finally, she purchased a home-testing kit for opiate use and made me take a drug test. When she saw that I was not giving up the drug, she started going to Al-Anon meetings and gave me an ultimatum: get clean or get out.

Turning Point: When my wife gave me the ultimatum. I knew I would lose my children. Plus, I was so miserable. I recall holding my baby boy in my arms and snorting OxyContin. I just started crying. I couldn't stand to look at myself in the mirror. I had been a successful businessman, had run marathons, and had a wonderful wife and kids. Now, I was so disgusted with what I had done to my life. Finally, I wanted to get better. I wanted treatment.

Advice to Others: If you are in the shape I was in, realize you need some long-term treatment. It *will* help you. Also, after treatment, get into a support group such as NA or AA. Don't try to do it alone. Link up with others in recovery who have gone through the same kind of ordeal. This kind of support is critical. And remember, the general public doesn't understand addiction. They just think you should stop being a scumbag and stop using drugs. If only it were that easy. They don't understand it is a disease and some of us will have to be vigilant about staying in recovery all our lives.

Beth, 49
Teacher

My first bout with addiction started innocently enough in 1986, when I fell and hurt my back. I was in and out of the hospital and went to a university hospital and to the Mayo Clinic. But nothing relieved my pain. I was told I would have to live with it. I was prescribed two Nubain shots a day, which I took for the next eight years. I always took two extra shots a day than was prescribed. This was a sign that I was inclined to chemical dependency, but I didn't realize it. At one point, another doctor put me in the hospital and I was taken off Nubain. Fortunately, I was able to come off this drug without any problems. Later, a therapist suggested I take yoga classes to help myself relax and ease the back pain. I did so, and within three months I felt less stress, and my back pain was gone.

A few years later, I was still free of back pain but was having migraine headaches, a chronic problem. I went to a neurologist who put me on the painkiller Stadol NS, a synthetic morphine. My pharmacist begged me not to take it; he knew the drug had high potential for addiction, but I told him I could handle it. After all, it was only one spray twice a day to help with the migraines. But, within a week, I was abusing Stadol NS. One spray quickly became two…then three and then four. I rationalized more of the medication would make me more free of pain. I could not leave my house without having to "spray up." At the same time, I was taking benzodiazepines every night to come down from the high of the day. The benzos had been prescribed by my psychiatrist several years earlier. I was also going to an emergency room once a week for Demerol because the Stadol was not working anymore for my headaches. It had only been four months, and I was an addict.

I also had started searching the aisles in drugstores. I was looking for other drugs that would help me escape my loneliness and depression. I bought over-the-counter drugs that would help me sleep. I was so very sick with my addiction at this time, but I could not see it. My only focus was getting my pills and my Stadol. I sunk further into depression; I had several stays in the mental health unit of our local hospital. I would be sent home with extra Stadol bottles. I would be in Stadol heaven for a few days.

My addiction had gotten so out of hand that my speech was always slurred. No one could understand me. My son stopped calling me and coming home from college. He couldn't understand my slurred speech, and I never really remembered what he had told me. I was pathetic. Yet I continued to drive myself places, praying all the time that I would not hit anyone or get a speeding ticket.

My husband and I were fighting often. He was fed up with my drug use. One night after a fight, I called my psychiatrist. He told me I had a drug problem and belonged in treatment. I told him I did not belong in treatment with "those addicts." But because I trusted the doctor, I went into treatment. It saved my life.

In detox I had a hard time coming off the benzos. I had never abused them, but I had taken them for years, so my body craved them. One moment I felt great and the next I felt as though my insides were being pulled out of me. My head felt like it was going to explode. But, I stuck it out for twelve days.

While in treatment, I was introduced to Narcotics Anonymous (NA). After I left treatment, I found the nearest NA meeting and have not stopped going. My clean date is May 27, 1997. I love my recovery and take it very seriously—I go to six to seven meetings a week. I have a sponsor, and I also sponsor three individuals. I have met many addicts who used prescriptions and tell me that NA saved their lives. My recovery has made me a much stronger person. I was a good eighteen months detoxing from the benzos. I had the hot sweats, cold sweats, and shakes. People in NA told me it would pass. I did start feeling better on a daily basis.

At seventeen months clean, I found out my husband was having an affair with someone he had met in an on-line chat room. I asked him to leave. That night I was going to buy beer and wine at a liquor store and then go hunting for drugs. However, I called my sponsor instead and she ordered me to a meeting that same night. She saved me from going back out. I now realize that nothing is worth relapsing over. I live by that motto today. It has kept me strong.

Even now, I avoid pain medications. I am so afraid of those drugs. I find alternative ways to deal with pain. When I am prescribed a drug, I question my physician and my pharmacist thoroughly about the medication. Plus, my doctors, pharmacist, and dentist all have the word *addict* in bright red letters on my files. It is my responsibility to keep them informed of my health history.

I have learned that I have a disease that is incurable. It can only be arrested. My disease is still very much alive and working in me. But, I am not using drugs. That is my freedom. I have a relationship with God, with my friends, and with my son and his wife. I am not married now. I divorced about a year ago.

I make it a point to remember my last day of using and how sick and out of control I was. The memory helps remind me of what depths I reached in just a few months. It also tells me that if I ever pick up again, I will get to that sick level faster and not be able to walk away from another active use. I may have that next high, but I sure do not have another recovery left in me. Narcotics Anonymous keeps me alive.

Turning Point: At the time, it was the ultimatum from my husband. When he threatened to leave me, I called my doctor and ultimately agreed with him that I should go for treatment.

Advice to Others: Don't be afraid to ask for help when you realize that you can't stop using. Get into treatment or Narcotics Anonymous as soon as you can. If you don't get into recovery you will lose everything.

Jeana, 29
Public Relations Director

I went to a Christian school. I never did drugs. I don't even take a drink. My ordeal with addiction came about as a result of chronic pain, which started when I was diagnosed with Crohn's disease at age 17. It's a chronic intestinal disorder that causes abdominal pain, cramping, fatigue, and diarrhea. The only treatment for me was surgery—I had to have my entire large bowel removed. I received an ileostomy, the surgical construction of a connection from the small bowel to the abdomen, which allows for the discharge of bodily waste.

I had abdominal pain, a lot of pain. So I was prescribed painkillers, Tylenol with Codeine and Percocet, which soon became my drug of choice. I didn't let anyone know that I was taking more than what was prescribed. By the time I was 20, I was an addict. I abused drugs for seven long years. I thought I needed these medications to function normally.

At one point, I moved to the Cleveland area and found my new physician was not as liberal in prescribing narcotics, so I began doctor shopping and making numerous visits to local emergency rooms. It was such a hassle to make doctor appointments and it was expensive, so I began writing my own prescriptions. On a recent visit to a doctor's office, I had noticed a black-and-white prescription pad on the

> *Addiction is a progressive disease—it will get worse. You've got to reach deep inside yourself if you want to get help. Otherwise, you'll meet with some kind of tragedy.*
>
> **Terry, 38**
> **In recovery**

desk. I figured the only other things I needed were his DEA number, a bottle of Liquid Paper, a black pen, and a copying machine and I was in business.

I started off writing a script for 30 pills and moved my way up to 90. I visited every pharmacy in town. It worked for about a month. And then I got caught. I remember the day. I had forgotten I had visited a particular pharmacy three days earlier and the pharmacist became suspicious. He called the doctor to verify the script and found it was fraudulent. He told me I was never to step foot in his pharmacy again. It scared me, but I was thankful I had gotten away with it...or so I thought. The next Saturday afternoon, about three days after my "incident" at the pharmacy, I received a phone call. I checked the caller ID and noticed the call was from a county office. My first thought was I didn't have any overdue books, so why would the county library be calling?

I answered the phone only to find a detective from the county sheriff's department on the other end of the line. As he was introducing himself, I was wracking my brain to come up with a good lie about the forged prescriptions. But somehow I knew he knew. I offered to go to his office immediately, but he suggested we wait until Wednesday. I thought, "Oh my God, I have to live with this up in the air for four long days?" I didn't know who to tell, if anyone. Finally, on Tuesday night I broke down and called my aunt, who's always been more like a sister to me. I begged her to accompany me.

We met the detective at his office. It was a cold February day. He took my aunt and me into his office. We introduced ourselves and before I could say anything else he was reading me my rights. I just started crying. I thought this couldn't be real. Oh, but it was very real. My aunt began to explain that my family was well aware I had a severe problem and that my Crohn's disease was the true cause for my addiction. He explained he needed to meet with his captain and the prosecutor to discuss what they were going to do. We were then escorted to the captain's office and were told what the legal repercussions were for what I had done. I could face twenty-four years in prison. Finally, they told me that given my health problems they would let me go, but warned if I ever repeated such a crime I would be charged for all the scripts I forged. Still, I didn't get sober right away. That would take time.

I went through rehab a total of four times in a nine-month period, but each time I came out of rehab and went back to using. In hindsight I think I looked at treatment as a cure—I would check in and the good doctors would fix me. I wasn't aware of the fact that recovery was something *I* had to do. The detoxification process each time went fairly smoothly. I always completed each aftercare program yet still couldn't suppress my overwhelming craving to self-medicate.

By now, I was at the peak of my addiction, and had developed a huge tolerance for my drugs. I was taking between 50 and 60 Percocets per day. I would do just about anything to obtain a prescription. I liked the idea of sobriety, but I loved the high more. In fact, I cared about my drugs more than my marriage—I was divorced from my husband of two years. And, I literally robbed family members of money and even raided their medicine cabinets for anything with a drowsiness sticker on the label. I stole money from my grandmother. I broke into our family business, stealing the cash box and credit cards. I had no boundaries. I was numb. I was eventually banned from all my family members' homes and lives.

I had nowhere to go, so I decided to run away to Florida. I was all alone. My family had always been there to pick up the pieces when I lived in Ohio. But now they refused to help me, financially or otherwise. I was holding down a job as a waitress in a casino, but I was still using. My life was actually worse. I was penniless and had no transportation. I couldn't break the cycle of abuse. I was too busy feeling sorry for myself and beating myself up for the mistakes I had made. I had dropped out of school, lost my marriage, friends, and family. And most importantly, I had lost myself.

I had hit bottom. I wanted a better life. I began doing some reading about addiction and realized that I wasn't so alone or so crazy. That same year my parents sent me a home Bible study for Christmas. I began doing a lesson every night. I was realizing that no matter how bad things had gotten I could at least try to make tomorrow better than today. I guess you could say I had a moment of clarity. If I had truly learned from the mistakes I had made I wouldn't make them again. I remember talking myself out of numerous doctors appointments to get more drugs. Sometimes, I was taking life minute by minute.

I realized I had to put into practice what I learned in rehab. It broke my heart to realize that one of the only memories I had of my mother was, with tears in her eyes, asking, "Where is that little girl I raised?" I didn't know. I didn't remember that girl. How could I find her again? I just wanted to be me. I wanted to be happy. I wanted to feel again. I had to take control of my life. I had to live up to my word to myself. I clung to my sobriety knowing no one could take it away from me. I knew how hard it was just to stay off the drugs. If I could stay sober I knew I could do just about anything. Inside I knew I was a survivor of my own war, the fight for my life and soul.

I had been clean for about a month when I took a big step and moved back to my hometown. Getting off the drugs was hard, but so was accepting responsibility for my actions and making amends with others. I approached each of my family members individually and apologized for my actions. I had to accept responsibility no matter how painful it was. Being around my family was uneasy for months.

I realize now that those three years I spent trying to get myself together they had been hurting, too. They felt as though they had failed me in some way when in reality I had been the selfish one. I didn't have answers to all their questions. I had to accept that I was an addict. I didn't know why I had chosen this for myself. I had to show them that this time I was really dedicated to making my life right. I remember a friend telling me he could tell I wasn't on drugs anymore because I actually had a personality again. Someone could really tell the difference. Finally! I began to reap the rewards of sobriety. That's when I knew I wanted to be clean and stay clean. I no longer had to worry about getting drugs and getting caught. I no longer had to look over my shoulder. I was truly free.

I am proud to say I have been sober for three years now. My relationship with my family is better than it's ever been. My mother and I speak to groups to help others who are struggling with addiction. We have made it our mission to shed the social stigmas of addiction. We are neither the first family nor the last to have suffered this pain. I attribute my successful recovery to the fact that I wanted it. I also had faith in God and I always knew my family loved me. I had to learn to love myself despite the consequences of my past.

> *I had to recover or I was going to lose my children. I was a zombie, in bed all day. I wanted to feel like a normal person and not always be thinking about how I would get my next pill.*
>
> Barbara, 39
> In recovery

Ironically, I learned during a visit to a pain clinic that the drugs I was taking were actually the reason for my discomfort. Percocet and other opiates actually immobilize the bowel at times, causing pain. I did not need the drugs to treat my original abdominal pain. I needed them to feed my addiction.

A gift that has come from my recovery is my continued relationship with the detective who arrested me. He became one of my biggest supporters and still is. When I would call the detective, he never judged me or questioned me. He just listened. His support meant so much to me because he was a stranger—he didn't have to like me. He seemed to actually empathize with my pain but didn't buy into my feeble excuses.

Turning Point: When I was in Florida all alone and realized that my life was a mess and I was the only one who could change it.

Advice to Others: Forgive yourself. Know that you are not alone. Understand that recovery takes complete dedication. Take each day second by second if you have to. There is comfort knowing that it is never too late. Quit trying to look back. Focus on your future. The only feelings you can change are your own. No one can change the past, but the future is yours. If you fall down, pick yourself up and try until you get it right. The hunger for pills can be overwhelming—it was all I could do not to run to the nearest ER and dupe some doctor into giving me what I wanted. The rewards of sobriety are endless. There is power in knowing deep down inside you can be accountable for your actions. Stop excusing your behavior and change it. Work on learning to be a respectable and trustworthy person again. Treat sobriety as something that is more valuable than all the riches in the world. No longer mourn for the person you once were or the innocence you have lost. Celebrate the person you are.

Margaret, 25
Homemaker

I knew nothing about prescription drug abuse. I'd never done any sort of drugs. But several years ago, I broke my arm and was given Vicodin for pain. I ended up going through a drug ordeal for about a year and a half. The Vicodin made me feel better—sort of a euphoria. I kept going back to the doctor and was getting prescriptions for 100 Vicodin with refills. No one told me the drug was addictive.

By the time my arm was getting better, I stopped taking the medication. But I would get really sick and would go to the emergency room with migraines. I never equated the drug with my headaches. At the emergency room, I would be given Vicodin. The headache would go away. I figured I had a migraine problem. So I continued the Vicodin for the headaches. I later realized that the headaches were from withdrawal from the drug.

Without the drug, within twenty-four hours I would have these really bad headaches again. I would try aspirin, but then I would start craving Vicodin. It was an addiction, a vicious circle. Then, once the drug had a hold of me, I wasn't living life on life's terms. Anytime something upset me, it would be an excuse to take more medication. I could forget about my problems much like an alcoholic would with liquor.

Because of my managed health-care plan, when I went to the doctor I rarely saw the same doctor. My addiction went undetected. When I finally did see my own doctor, he told me I had a dependency problem. I'd been taking Vicodin for a year and a half, and it was only toward the end of this time that I realized that the pills, not the headaches, were my problem.

Then I had to go through a drug detox. It was an outpatient program; I had two kids to take care of. I was given other medications to help ease the discomfort. But, for about seven days I stayed in my bedroom—I couldn't function at all. I couldn't sleep. I had memory problems. I was exhausted. I had no energy to do anything.

For about four months, I went to personal counseling, to AA meetings, and to a prescription drug abuse class. Every day was a struggle. I had to learn how to live life all over again. I am still afraid of relapsing. I'm horrified of ever having an injury or surgery for which I might need pain medication. I think what really upsets me is that I was never warned that I was getting a highly addictive drug. I didn't have a clue.

Turning Point: I was tired of being sick. Through groups and treatment I learned to make myself feel better in different ways. I started exercising a lot. I jogged and walked. I bought a StairMaster. It made me feel a lot better. I started focusing on me, taking care of my emotional needs.

Advice to Others: There is light at the end of the tunnel. It may take a while, but hang in there.

Billy, 72
Physician

I was about 27, in my residency training for medical school, when I had a painful kidney stone attack. I was given an injection of codeine. Never in all my life had I felt the feeling that drug gave me. The euphoria was just incredible. I stored that in my memory bank and then every time I had a kidney stone attack—and I had many—I would ask for a shot of codeine. Then the kidney stone attacks subsided, and I was getting on with my life and my medical practice.

Later, in my forties, I had a series of health problems and had to have several surgeries—for a lumbar disk, cervical disk, my knee, and later my right hip. I would be given painkillers after each surgery, and I would extend my usage of the drugs. I managed to always con the doctors into giving me a little extra. Gradually, I increased my use of the drugs and became a full-fledged addict.

During a ten-year period, two of my drugs of choice were Dilaudid and Demerol—both powerful painkillers. I never prescribed for myself since that was illegal, but I used samples from drug companies. I also received drugs from those who'd had a death in the family; they would call me and ask me what to do with pain medications after their loved ones died. I would tell them to drop off the drugs at my office. It's sad, but true.

At one point, I was also injecting drugs. I had read that in times of emergency, one could inject a patient through the clothing without having to get the patient undressed. That's all I needed to read. I began injecting myself through my clothing. It was quicker, more convenient. As a result, I would often have blood on my pants or lab coat when I was in the office. Every time someone said, "Oh, there's blood on you," I'd say, "Oh, I must have spilled some blood in the lab." Looking back, I was crying for help and nobody heard me. I was hooked. I had to have drugs. As with most addicts, I no longer got the rush from the drugs, like I did early on. I needed the drugs to maintain, to keep from getting sick.

Eventually, as a result of injecting myself through clothing, I got a serious blood infection. When my physician asked me about the infection, I told him I had been injecting myself for pain. Even then, I really didn't consider myself an addict. I was still in deep denial.

During the course of years I was addicted, I destroyed many relationships—both personal and in business. I managed to do no harm to my medical practice until the very end of my addiction days.

Turning Point: I got into trouble with the law. I was busted by two undercover narcotic agents who came to my office because they noticed my excessive prescribing for other patients. I had prescribed Valium for two undercover agents. Arrested as I was coming back from lunch, I was handcuffed and paraded through my office full of patients and put in jail. The arrest saved my life. I got into treatment in 1997. Since then, I've worked the 12 steps of recovery in AA, and have reached out to be of service to other people.

> *Going to 12-step meetings fills up the "black hole" in my heart. I find people who are like me, and we can talk openly.*
>
> Michael, 56
> In recovery

Advice to Others: Get to a physician who specializes in addiction. That's number one—find a doctor who understands what you're going through. Also recognize that you are powerless over the world around you—powerless over people and places. This is the first of the twelve steps of recovery. You have to realize that you cannot control everything in your life. Only then can you regain control of your life. It's also important to realize that your anger, fears, and shame are all generated by your own brain. Recovery can help you cope with these.

Michelle, 31

Businesswoman

I had no experience with drugs—illegal or legal. I'd never even heard of most of the prescriptions I ended up taking. After graduating from college, I started working for a large corporation.

I got promoted to the position of computer system specialist. I was young and had a lot of responsibility, including oversight of thirty-seven sales reps and their budgets. I liked it, but it was more pressure than I was used to.

I started getting really bad headaches and went to my doctor. At the first appointment the doctor prescribed Fiorinal, which I later learned is a narcotic. Within a few weeks, my headaches were continuing and so I started getting injections of Demerol, which I had never heard of. I had a standing prescription to go into the doctor's office and have the nurse give me a shot of Demerol.

I know now that it is a Schedule II narcotic like morphine.

Soon, however, I was having the headaches daily, to the point of needing to get the injections. I'd have headaches without them. But I was really getting worse and worse headaches. My family started getting really worried about me. We thought something was very wrong. I would wake up in the mornings, shaking and vomiting. I didn't realize I was having withdrawal from the Demerol.

My family had never been around drug users, so we didn't know that my symptoms were actually drug withdrawal. The doctors were writing down my symptoms, but no one seemed to suspect drug withdrawal from an opiate. Often, I got the shots from nurses and never saw a doctor. I still didn't connect the medication with what I thought was an illness. I was getting sicker and sicker and the medication wasn't helping. So my family insisted that I be hospitalized for tests. During that hospital stay I was on an IV, and I was to the point by now of ordering the Demerol myself. I knew just exactly what I needed in order to feel better. I'd tell the nurse, "I need 100 milligrams of Demerol every two to three hours." They were giving it to me.

A year earlier, I'd never even heard of Demerol and now I knew how to order it. I was asking for it IM (intramuscularly) or IV (intravenously) with Vistaril or with Phenergan. Vistaril, a sedative, acted like a kicker and made the Demerol last longer. Phenergan was an anti-nausea drug. I knew just exactly what I wanted.

Then, within a three-day period, I'd had over a gram of Demerol, and I had a grand mal seizure. I remember waking up with two doctors and a nurse in the room with me. I had blood in my mouth and all over my shirt. They told me I had seizured.

So, I was never diagnosed with any illness. My problem was Demerol. So from there, I had to go into chemical dependence recovery. My family put me in a care unit. There, at first, I thought I was completely out of place. I was in with addicts who were talking about "highballs" and "eight balls," things I had no knowledge of. My attitude was that I just needed to get my life back on track and be done with doctors and drugs, but that was not the case. My doctor in the care unit said I was the worst case of detox he'd seen from legal or illegal drugs. I was in detox seven days longer than some of the heroin addicts.

My denial was really high, because I didn't think I was truly an addict. I just thought my other doctors had put me on too much medication. But I had to finally say, "I'm responsible for my recovery today and regardless of how I got here, I'm here." Being angry didn't really help me.

Demerol is like heroin. It's very hard to stop taking. I did finish my inpatient treatment and then started going to support groups. But I still felt out of place; I didn't think these meetings were what I needed. A lot of prescription drug addicts feel out of place in 12-step meetings. In Narcotics Anonymous they were talking about illegal drugs and at AA meetings they were talking about alcohol, so I had a hard time fitting in. That just fed my denial. I could say, "None of this fits for me." I heard only the differences, not the similarities.

So I went back to work, against my doctor's advice. He told me, "Your problem is no longer headaches, your problem is about surviving. People die from this." He really wanted me to have more recovery.

But I went back to work and went out one night with friends and had a few drinks. I'd never had a drinking problem so I didn't think there was any danger. But within hours of taking a couple of drinks, my craving for Demerol was back. That's how quickly it happened. I relapsed.

I felt really hopeless then. In AA you hear people talking about hitting the "bottom," when you feel like you can't live with the drugs but you can't live without them. I hated the way I was living. I opted to keep taking the drugs and to make myself be happy. I went to the Caribbean on vacation and tried to tell myself I was okay. But it didn't take me long to end up feeling really hopeless. I knew I couldn't go on that way.

So then, I was hospitalized two or three times in psych wards; my family intervened—they wanted to help. Yet, I was angry and yelling at them. It seemed like everything that had been important to me in life was no longer important. The only thing that mattered was not feeling sick from the drugs but at the same time wanting them so I could feel normal. That was all that mattered. I was angry and bitter about everything.

Turning Point: I took two bottles of pills—a suicide attempt. I woke up in a medical center. And maybe it was grace from above, but somehow when I woke up I felt like maybe I could get help. I remembered meeting people in support groups who, like me, had been in trouble with prescription drugs. I had a bit of hope. I thought I could return to the 12-step groups for help. I started going back to AA meetings and Narcotics Anonymous.

Advice to Others: I came to realize that I was worth getting better. And every single person in that situation is. I held onto that. I found help in 12-step meetings. I found help in dealing with all my resentments about what had happened to me. I had a lot of guilt and shame, too. The support groups helped me find a way to deal with that and learn to take better care of myself. I had a supportive family, but still I had to do the work. They couldn't do it for me. I suggest reaching out to people. Learn to trust others.

Don, 51

Realtor

I've been recovering from pill addiction for several years. In my support group, I see people going through the same kinds of experiences today.

A few years ago, I was waking up very early each morning, and it was really causing fatigue. So, I started with a sleeping pill called Dalmane, a benzodiazepine. At first, I took the drug as needed. Later on I took it every night at the insistence of my doctor. He said it couldn't hurt me. It worked like magic for five or six months, then I started waking up early again in the morning. I couldn't sleep.

Then, over the next two weeks, I became severely depressed and my short-term memory was terrible. I had anxiety. I lost my sense of taste. I couldn't figure out what my problem was. I suspected the pills, but my doctor assured me it couldn't be and sent me to a psychiatrist.

But on my own, I stopped taking the drug. I realize now, looking back, I went into a serious withdrawal. I was having terrible depression and couldn't sleep. I started seeing a series of doctors and specialists, trying to find out what was wrong.

By now, I had been off the medication for a few weeks and told my doctor I had suspected the pills were my problem. He explained that the pills had a half-life of 10 days—in other words, the drug would have been out of my system by then. I'd been off it for a few weeks.

So I tried antidepressants and psychiatrists. Nothing seemed to make me any better. Then I ran into a psychiatrist who put me back on a benzodiazepine, Ativan, and two or three other drugs. I did improve dramatically within a few days. I then stayed on these medications for years, up until 1990.

During these years, I took myself off the benzos a couple of times. But a few weeks later, the depression would hit me again. The doctor, who I would only see two or three times a year, would reinforce the fact that I needed the medication. So I'd go back on it.

By 1990, my business and family life was going downhill. That's when I was put on another benzo, and that experience became my moment of truth. The first night I took the drug I went through the worst panic attack of my life. It was the most god-awful emotional state I've ever been in. That told me that something was terribly wrong with my medication.

I searched for a few months and by the end of 1990, I found a doctor who was an addiction specialist. I also got into a support group. I did an outpatient detox. I was put on Klonopin and tapered off in twelve weeks. It was probably too fast, and it was really difficult. Life was awful and I was suicidal. I should have taken an antidepressant, but by that time I was too afraid of drugs. Now, I've been drug free for several years. (I'm diabetic so I take insulin. That's all.)

Turning Point: The night I had the severe panic attack. That's when I knew I had to get help, and I was determined to survive.

Advice to Others: Realize that you need help with these dependencies. You cannot do it alone. Find a knowledgeable doctor—one who understands what's going on with you—and find a support group. It's essential to talk to other people who have gone through what you're going through.

Justin, 37
Attorney

I dislocated my shoulder and broke my wrist by falling down a set of stairs. It affected the nerves that ran into my neck, head, and jaw, so I had intense pain. Then came my first exposure to pain medication.

After a while, I told the doctor that my medication, Codeine no. 3, was not stopping the pain. He said to take two. After a couple of months, when the pain persisted, my doctor gave me Codeine no. 4, which was twice the strength of the no. 3. So I was getting 120 milligrams per dose, prescribed for four hours apart. I would use the medication as needed, but was gradually using it more and more. Dependency was kicking in. My tolerance was building and I really didn't realize how much I was using it. It was a very gradual thing. It never occurred to me that I had a drug problem.

Two years later my jaw pain continued, so I went to a different medical center for tests and x-rays. I was told I had a problem with my jaw and needed surgery. However, my insurance plan would not pay for it.

So my doctors said we could only treat the pain. I told my physician that I thought I was dependent on the codeine. I knew I had a tolerance built up and if I didn't take the medication I would feel sick. I was afraid that I was becoming dependent. My doctor said it's not unusual to need ongoing medication for pain management, so I was sent to a special department for treatment. There, I was given Vicodin, which was more potent than what I was taking.

Within a couple of weeks, I was really needing the drug. Every time I went back to see my doctor I would tell him I needed more pills. So I would get more. Then, I was switched to Percocet and would get occasional shots of Demerol or morphine suppositories. I also had muscle relaxants and tranquilizers.

With the opiate drugs, you build a tolerance, so others don't readily notice you're on a drug. You just need it to keep from getting sick. However, I now realize my behavior was changing. I wasn't dealing with life normally. I would be jubilant sometimes, deeply depressed other times. My motivation to do things was affected. I managed to adjust my dosages so I could function at work, but I did call in sick a lot. I was having problems in my marriage—we eventually got divorced. I had no idea my problems were related to drug use. I just thought I was suffering from depression.

A couple of years later, I overdosed. I had received a shot of Demerol and came home and took tranquilizers. I went to sleep and woke up and took more tranquilizers. I was never really aware of how many pills I was taking. It is quite common, once your judgment is impaired, to not realize how many more pills you're taking. That same night, when I started to take even more pills, I did realize the bottle of 100 tablets was nearly empty. I got really scared. I knew I was not feeling right. I called 911. When the ambulance got there, I was delirious. I ended up in the intensive care unit and almost died.

Once I got out of the hospital, I got my prescriptions refilled and started all over again. I knew the drugs were a problem, but every single day was a major effort for me to try to quit. I had to have the drugs. I would get 150 milligrams of Demerol in a shot and then take Percodan.

I was feeding a real drug habit now. I tried several times to get treatment and go through detox, but then I'd still have real physical pain in my neck. Finally a few months later, I went to a specialist who performed surgery on my neck—fixed my physical problem—and that helped me get over my drug addiction. With treatment, I got my life together.

Looking back, it seems the medical community didn't want to take time to explain the nature of addictive drugs. Still, it's important that they prescribe painkillers when a patient needs them. I've seen that problem with my mother who legitimately needed pain medication but couldn't get it because her doctors were too cautious. I've seen both extremes. There needs to be balance.

Turning Point: Personal realization. By the time I was taking drugs every day for three months in a row, I knew I was in trouble. I thought I could stop myself at first, but I couldn't. When I realized I couldn't stop, the more scared I became. But I was also afraid that I couldn't live without the drugs.

I fought that fear for a year before I finally went for inpatient treatment. I was in for thirty days. I relapsed several times. I went back to inpatient treatment seven times, ranging from five days to five weeks. To this day, seven years later, I still go to AA meetings two or three times a week.

Advice to Others: The first thing I would say is, realize you can live without the drugs. I had become 100 percent convinced that I could not live without them. I thought it was great that other people could recover, but I was so addicted that I thought there was no way in hell I could function without the drugs.

If someone is dependent, they may have to take a giant leap of faith and realize that they can live life without drugs. It takes some time, and it's good to join a support group of people who are going through the same thing. Pair up with someone who has used a similar drug—they'll know exactly what you've gone through. Stick with these people who have been through it, and recovery can work for you.

Terry, 37
Nurse

I'm a nurse who ended up taking drugs on the job. This kind of abuse is rampant in hospitals all over the country. A lot of nurses need help. In one of my support groups, seven out of thirteen of us are nurses. The medical profession is so intense. You're so afraid of doing something wrong. There's a lot of pressure on medical professionals, and we have access to the drugs. Sometimes, we want to help others and do everything perfectly. That's a lot of pressure. We're only human.

My problem started when I was a nurse on a psych ward. I was injured when an enraged patient attacked me. I suffered a neck injury, and I was prescribed Vicodin. Eventually I had to have carpal tunnel surgery and a thumb fusion from the injury. I was on Vicodin for two years.

I loved the drug. It was wonderful. Life was easier. My husband was abusive, but when I was on the drug, whatever he did or said didn't bother me as much.

I built up a tolerance to the drug. I started taking one every three or four hours, then I'd take two. After a while, I was taking 20 pills, a day. Being a nurse, I knew this wasn't right. But no one knew I was taking so many pills. The only change in me was that my emotions had become really flat.

By now, I was working in a long-term care unit and I was taking the hospital's drugs myself, signing charts as if patients were receiving them. I was the charge nurse. I had the key to the narcotics cabinet. I'd just write on a patient's chart that they'd taken a certain medication, and I took it instead. The DEA requires that the drugs be recorded on a narcotics sheet, so I'd sign out the drugs to a patient. I'd write down some excuse, that the patient had a headache or back pain. Then I'd take the drugs. It was easy. This went on for a year and a half. No one ever knew.

Later, I worked in a doctor's office, where drug samples were available from drug salespeople. These samples were never registered, so no one knew I was taking them. Once again, I had the key to the drug cabinet. I was taking Vicodin, Xanax, Restoril, Ativan, and Tylenol with Codeine.

I knew I was an addict, but thought since I was a nurse, I could stop on my own. I really tried, but I couldn't. No way. Had I stopped cold, I would have had a seizure and maybe died.

Eventually, I was phoning pharmacies with my own prescriptions—100 Vicodin a week. I worked for six doctors, so I would use their names, say I was calling from their office and order a script for Terry. I used five or six pharmacies. It was easy.

I was always preoccupied with getting pills. Anytime I started to run out of drugs, I would panic. I kept track on my watch: was it time to take a pill?

The end came when I got busted at work. One of the doctors caught on that I was calling different pharmacies. That was on a Friday. I was fired. I was so humiliated, really ashamed. I considered suicide, but having two children made me realize I couldn't do that. So I admitted I needed help. I didn't want the drugs, but my body did. I could not stop. I knew I was dying. I was anorexic. I was so thin I couldn't even sit on a chair because my bones were sticking out. I'd lost 73 pounds. I knew I was going to die. In my mind, death was the only way to be free of the addiction. In fact, when you're that addicted, the cells in your body turn to the drug as their food. You don't feel like you need regular food or anything else—just that drug. If you take the drug away, it's like starving yourself to death.

So, I called a patient from our office who I knew was in recovery. She knew exactly what I needed. By Monday, I was in drug treatment. I was in detox for 15 days. The first couple of days were okay, because I was being given drugs, but then my doses were gradually reduced. I couldn't sleep. I would shake. Just remembering what the physical withdrawal was like would keep me from ever relapsing. I ached all over. Muscle cramps. Diarrhea. Vomiting. My body screamed for the pills.

Once I was through detox, I had to start dealing with the emotional issues that caused me to drug myself in the first place, and those issues were right there, staring me in the face. I fought the feelings like crazy because I'd been through a lot of abuse in my life and I just didn't want to feel any of the buried pain I was going to have to face. I made it, but I would not have made it without the rehab center. I wouldn't have made it at home. I would have relapsed. The first 90 days are not easy.

I was blessed with a wonderful sponsor in my support group. She told me life would get better and that I deserved it. I started to believe it even though it took me a while because I had been abused much of my life. I do believe in God, and my faith helped me.

Once I got out of inpatient treatment, I was scared to death, scared I would relapse. I went to two and three meetings (both AA and Narcotics Anonymous) a day for the first 90 days. That's how I did it. AA had more people with more years of sobriety, plus the structure there was good for me. In Narcotics Anonymous, the people expressed a lot of love. I needed both. I had to reach out.

Being in recovery, I can't believe how good I feel. I would have never thought I could feel so happy inside. I look forward to life. I was even hired back at the doctor's office where I was fired. I still go through rough times, but when I do, I call my sponsor and I get to a meeting. I wish everyone could have the luxury of a support system like I have. All these people will help you, but you have to reach out. You do have to make that effort. You have to be willing.

Turning Point: Getting busted at work was definitely the turning point for me.

Advice to Others: Be totally honest with everyone—your friends, your therapist, and your family. Admit that your life is screwed up and that you need help. Realize you're not perfect. I found it's really neat being "not perfect." Realizing I was just another human took the weight of the world off my shoulders. Today I have freedom, love, and hope in my life. It's amazing. And it gets better every day.

Caroline, 50
Actress

I'm a wife and a mother, and I've been an actress for twenty-five years, working mostly in television shows and commercials. I was addicted to Xanax and nearly lost everything.

I went to only one doctor, one pharmacist. I could get 50 to 100 Xanax on Monday, and if I wanted 100 more on Friday I could get them. Benzodiazepines, as central nervous system depressants, can not only cause physical damage, but can affect your mind, your judgment. They affected my mind and my emotional well-being.

I started taking the drug after becoming extremely claustrophobic after being trapped in my room on a train, in a train accident on my way east. A psychiatrist prescribed Xanax and I took it, knowing very little about the drug. I take responsibility for taking the pills, but I also want doctors to take responsibility and to acknowledge that some of them have problems with misprescribing.

I was chemically dependent on Xanax for over two years. After being on the drug for nine months, my panic attacks were worse. These pills can boomerang on you. My initial symptoms returned with a vengeance. This recurrence of original symptoms is called a rebound effect.

I didn't know it then, but I was building up a tolerance. I began taking more and more. I was so sick from taking the drug that I couldn't drive to work. I couldn't work. I wasn't able to take care of my children. I wasn't able to be a wife to my husband. I was isolating and withdrawing.

This dependency took away my dreams and my belief in myself—things I'd worked for all my life. Looking back, I see that my therapist and psychiatrist seemed uneducated about the dangers of this drug. They said I would have no problem getting off it. But from the shape I was in, I knew in my heart and my soul that something was terribly wrong.

I entered a treatment center in August of 1987, a shell of the woman I once was. My entire stay was 40 days. I was in detox, withdrawing for 12 days. I remember seeing people coming to the treatment center who were addicted to heroin, crack, ice, cocaine, and alcohol, and they were out of the detox part in three days. They were walking down the halls, strong and in command. I would watch these people as I was crawling down the same hallway. I had temporarily lost my ability to walk.

I've been off Xanax for nineteen years, and I'm alive today because I'm one of the fortunate ones. I am strong today. In 1989, in Los Angeles, I co-founded Benzodiazepines Anonymous (see Resources), a 12-step group for those recovering from addiction to benzodiazepines.

Turning Point: When I knew that I was ill, yet I could not stop taking the pills.

Advice to Others: Ask your doctor questions about the drugs you're getting. It's your body. It's your brain. Be knowledgeable about your medications. Don't just put yourself out there for a doctor to take care of you. Prepare yourself—it's vital.

Barbara, 38
Homemaker

My addiction started as a result of an injury. I hurt my back at work, picking up a heavy box. I had surgery on my neck and wore three different braces, and even though I eventually took off the braces, the pain would not go away.

I was given Tylenol with Codeine. I also had Darvon and Vicodin. Then, the addiction cycle kicked in. I had mood swings; I was either very high or very low. I couldn't understand what was happening.

> *You are not alone. Addiction is a very treatable illness. It is not about shame. There is help.*
>
> Sharon Hartman
> Caron Foundation

Before long, I was taking 10 pills a day. I kept a diary and noticed that I was soon up to 12 a day, then 15. By the time I was taking 25 a day, I knew I was addicted. I was a recovering alcoholic and had been sober for five years, but I knew I was addicted.

The pills began to "talk" to me. I was taking them every 20 minutes, then every 15 minutes, finally every 10 minutes. When I told my doctor who had prescribed all these drugs what had happened, she dropped me as a patient. She was a neurosurgeon. She told me to get an MD.

I called some women I knew from recovery groups, telling them that the pills were in charge of me and that I was dying. I couldn't tell the difference between the pain in my back and my psychological pain.

I went to another doctor and he gave me 90 pills of Tylenol with Codeine. I realized I was in trouble. The doctors I was seeing didn't understand addiction.

I couldn't stop taking the pills. So, I got into a hospital treatment program and was in for 20 days. I hit bottom in the hospital. I was very sick. I was vomiting. If I drank even an ounce of water I would throw up. My lowest point was when I was lying on the bathroom floor with the dry heaves.

Turning Point: The shots I was getting in detox to stop the dry heaves really burned when I got them in the hip. After about 20 of them I literally cried at the thought of getting another one. I remember falling to the bathroom floor, begging the nurses not to give me another shot. I cried and cried and cried. I prayed like I'd never prayed before, admitting to God that I'd been an alcoholic and was now an addict and to please help me.

Advice to Others: Talk to your pharmacist to find out if a drug is addictive. Ask how long you should take it. A pharmacist will give you a lot of information if you ask for it. It's also good to get a second opinion from another doctor. If you've had alcohol or drug problems, tell your doctor right up front. The opiate drugs can hook you so quickly.

Get support through AA or Narcotics Anonymous. There's a lot of wisdom in those groups. They have a lot of knowledge about different drugs and how they can affect you.

3

Treatment for Addiction

Geoff, a 36-year-old man, checked himself into a treatment facility. He was able to admit he had a drug problem, but still, he wasn't sure treatment would help him. With tears streaming down his cheeks, he told the psychiatrist, "I've had these problems all my life. I have no reason to believe you can make them go away. I don't think anyone can help me."

The psychiatrist listened.

"I feel so needy," Geoff continued. "I have this emptiness, this 'hole' in my heart."

"We are all needy," the psychiatrist responded. "We humans are unlike most other creatures on this earth. We all become dependent and needy. You are not unusual."

Now Geoff listened.

"We can help you," the psychiatrist told him. "Tens of thousands of people recover every year. Treatment works. If it didn't, we'd all be out of business."

Geoff continued treatment successfully.

Treatment Works

There is no "one-size-fits-all" approach to treating addiction. Treatment depends on individual needs and circumstances and the drug involved. But, for any type of treatment for chemical dependency, the goal is to help individuals make changes in their lives so that they need not continue to depend on drugs for coping. In turn, their lives are richer and more constructive. Treatment involves learning to make changes in thinking and behaving. Today, most forms of treatment will also involve the use of medications to ease the transition into drug-free living.

Medical Detoxification

Many individuals require *medical detoxification* before they can begin a program of treatment or rehabilitation. The purpose of detoxification, or "detox" as it is commonly called, is to help individuals withdraw from an addictive substance. Detox is conducted under close medical supervision during the withdrawal phase. Withdrawal symptoms may range from mild irritability to seizures and even death. Other common withdrawal symptoms include anxiety, panic, depression, incoherent thoughts, muscle cramps, vomiting, and nausea.

When patients first enter a detox unit, they are typically given a physical exam and their medical history is taken. Health professionals are looking for any other underlying physical problems as well as the drug history. It's important for physicians to learn what drugs the patient has been taking and for how long. Then, to ease the symptoms of withdrawal, patients may be given tranquilizers, anti-hypertensive drugs, or other medications. Some patients may be given small doses of the drug to which they're addicted with the intent of gradually tapering the doses.

Detox usually takes several days, perhaps longer, depending on the type of drug to which one is addicted. Some treatment centers have their own medical unit for detoxing. If not, an individual may be referred to an area hospital.

Some detox centers are active in providing individual and group counseling sessions during the time an individual is in the detox unit; other medical units may not offer emotional support. Once the detox is complete, patients are better prepared to enter treatment.

Inpatient Treatment

Inpatient treatment, in which an individual stays in a residential treatment center, is often based on the "Minnesota Model." This model of treatment involves three to six weeks at an inpatient treatment facility, followed by extended outpatient therapy in such support groups as Narcotics Anonymous or Alcoholics Anonymous.

Once admitted for inpatient treatment, individuals are usually assigned a primary counselor who will oversee their treatment program. During the inpatient stay, individuals are asked to participate in both individual and group therapy. Treatment programs also may include watching instructional videotapes, listening to lectures, writing assignments, reading materials on recovery, and attending 12-step meetings. The goal is to teach individuals how to live without drugs and how to avoid situations that could lead to a relapse. For example, individuals may learn to carefully select the types of company they keep or the places they visit. Does the individual live in a drinking and drugging environment? If so, plans may need to be made to avoid these settings. Does the recovering person avoid reaching out to other people for help? If so, isolation after treatment may trigger a relapse. During treatment, one may identify personality or character issues that may put the individual at risk for relapse.

In short, treatment serves as an education to help the patient answer several key questions: What am I doing to myself emotionally and physically with drugs? What will happen if I continue this habit? How can I stop using drugs? What can I do to stay stopped?

These are the kinds of questions Scott, a 40-year-old man from the East Coast, began asking himself as he entered a treatment facility.

"I had tried treatment before, but this last time it worked because I wanted recovery this time. Before, I went into treatment for others—my wife and relatives. But this time I wanted it for myself. I had hit bottom, and I didn't want to live like that anymore. Drugs had robbed me of so much—my business, my family—everything I had worked for. I didn't give treatment a chance before. This last time time I did what the professionals told me. I did not try to run my program.

"I'm also learning that I am not just weak. I'm not beating myself up emotionally so much because I understand now that I have a disease. It's taken me twenty-five years to learn that."

Choosing a Treatment Center

Just as it is important to choose a reputable hospital for any other illness, it is important to choose an addiction treatment center that operates at the hands of qualified personnel. Sharon Hartman is Program Director for Adult Extended Services at the Caron Foundation, Wernersville, PA, the nation's largest addiction treatment center and also one of the oldest. She recommends patients and families ask treatment center staff the following questions when considering a treatment center for chemical dependency:

- Is there a physician on staff who has been trained in addiction medicine?
- Do therapists have training and credentials in addiction treatment?
- Is auxiliary treatment available for family members? Recovery is much enhanced if family members understand the dynamics of addiction in a family.
- Does the treatment center teach about relapse? Addiction is prone to relapse, and individuals can learn how to manage it.
- Does the treatment program teach new ways to manage stress? If drugs are no longer used to cope with stress, it's important to develop new coping methods and skills.
- Are 12-step programs included? These are among the oldest and most successful recovery programs.
- Does the treatment program help individuals incorporate spirituality into their lives? For some, spirituality may involve religion, but spirituality also refers to all principles that enhance one's sense of purpose and meaning in life.

Outpatient Treatment

In an outpatient treatment program, the patient does not stay overnight at the treatment facility. In many cases, the patient may carry out routine activities during the day—going to work or to school—and then attend treatment programs in the evening.

Treatment may involve several hours once or twice a week, or it may require every night of the week.

The treatment regimen usually involves sessions similar to those of an inpatient program—therapy sessions, a primary counselor, participating in group counseling sessions, listening to lectures and tapes, and attending 12-step meetings. Individuals who are very motivated are often considered better candidates for outpatient treatment since it provides more "opportunities" for the patient to relapse.

> *Individuals have a better chance of staying in recovery if they also receive treatment for their underlying emotional problems, such as depression.*
>
> David Oslin, M.D.
> Center of Studies on Addiction
> University of Pennsylvania

Partial Day Hospital Programs

As insurance companies have tightened guidelines on the amount of payment they'll provide for inpatient treatment, an increasing number of treatment centers have developed *partial day hospital programs*. Here, patients participate in a treatment program throughout the day, returning home at night. For example, some centers run programs in which patients arrive at the facility Monday through Friday at 8:30 A.M. and stay until 9:00 P.M. The treatment programs vary in length, with some lasting two to three weeks. During this time patients are involved in such activities as individual and group counseling, 12-step meetings, and a variety of lectures. The lectures might cover such topics as nutrition, how addiction affects the mind and body, intimacy, sexuality, spirituality, stress, and relapse prevention.

A partial day hospital program might also set up modified programs for individuals who are unable to attend the full-day sessions all week. For example, these individuals may be set up with "half a program," in which they are involved in the treatment program for three to six hours a day.

Follow-Up Care

Many treatment centers offer *follow-up care*, often called, *aftercare*. These programs are designed to help prevent relapse in patients who have completed their primary treatment program. Aftercare typically involves individual or group counseling, or both, to provide emotional and spiritual support once or twice a week. The length of aftercare programs ranges from several months to one or two years.

Virtually all treatment programs advocate participation in 12-step programs, both during aftercare and once aftercare has ended. Twelve-step groups include such organizations as Narcotics Anonymous (NA) and Alcoholics Anonymous (AA). The success of such groups is attributed, in part, to the power of the "group dynamic," or the emotional and spiritual support that the members give each other. Consistent participation in these groups helps individuals from isolating themselves, and also nourishes them emotionally and spiritually by helping them "get outside" of themselves by helping others. Both these dynamics are considered helpful in preventing relapse.

Rapid Detox Treatment for Opiate Addiction

Rapid detox centers began appearing in the United States in the mid-1990s. As the name implies, the detoxification is completed rapidly, ridding the patient of cravings and withdrawal symptoms within a matter of hours rather than over a period of days in a conventional treatment center. Done while the patient is under general anesthesia, rapid detox treatment is only for opiate addiction. The cost of the treatment may range from $4,000 to $10,000.

The Detox Procedure

One treatment program, offering the rapid detox, is located at Texas Tech University Health Sciences Center. Patients are chosen only after careful screening and must demonstrate a desire to get off the opiates. The treatment is carried out in the intensive care unit, where body and brain wave activity can be monitored.

"Before we put patients to sleep we give them a drug which neutralizes the body's ability to become hyper or aroused, explains Dr. Alan Kaye, who heads the rapid detox program. "Once we're ready to begin, the patient is given a general anesthetic. Then, we give the patient a massive amount of an opiate *antagonist*, or a drug that blocks the opiate." Then over a six-hour period, while the patient is asleep, he or she goes through withdrawal. "Essentially, all the opiates are wiped off the brain's receptor sites. It's done humanely because the patient is not awake."

When the individual awakens, he or she is given another opiate blocker, which is taken orally for six months. This drug is intended to decrease cravings and block an opiate from having any affect if the individual should relapse.

Another component of the treatment is counseling. Arrangements are made before the procedure, for patients to see a therapist, psychologist, psychiatrist, or an addictionologist to help patients deal with psychosocial issues. According to Kaye, "Everyone has complex psychosocial issues and it's a critical link for success to address these issues. Otherwise, there is a greater chance for relapse. The better the psychosocial counseling, the higher the success rates for staying in recovery."

Is the Treatment Safe?

Although thousands of successful rapid detox procedures have been performed in the United States, the safety of the treatment is still the subject of controversy. Some medical and addiction specialists say there is risk of death any time general anesthesia is used. The American Society of Addiction Medicine states that additional research should be completed to confirm both the procedure's efficacy and safety. According to ASAM, most of the procedure's risk is related to the experience and expertise of the anesthesiologist and other medical personnel carrying out the procedure.

Relapse Prevention

Relapse refers to an individual's return to drug use, after a period of abstinence. If you or someone in your life has a relapse, don't give up. Addiction is a chronic disease and many recovering individuals experience relapses before sustaining sobriety. A "slip" may be discouraging, but it should never be considered the end of recovery.

"There is no such thing as a hopeless addict. There are only those who haven't found out about relapse prevention techniques," according to Terence T. Gorski, a nationally recognized recovery and relapse prevention specialist. "Learning how to be sober is a skill-training experience. You have to learn to depend on something besides alcohol or drugs to deal with your thoughts, feelings, relationships and behaviors. Basically, relapse prevention therapy is based upon the premise that there are observable warning signs that occur before a person returns to alcohol or drug use."

According to Gorski, most relapses can be attributed to the "triggers" outlined below:

- Stress or change occurs in a person's life.
- The stressor triggers a change in thinking. The individual begins using old, addictive thinking strategies, which then trigger a change in feeling.
- The individual begins to experience painful, distressful, unmanageable feelings.
- These feelings produce a change in behavior. The person begins using self-defeating or compulsive behaviors to cope with the feelings.
- The individual starts associating with people, places, and things that tolerate his or her self-destructive behavior.

With the Gorski model in mind, what should you do to prevent relapse? First, identify your own unique pattern of relapse warning signs. Every recovering person has relapse warning signs. They are like fingerprints—everybody has them, but each person's are different. Write down your list of relapse warning signs and describe how they move you from stable recovery back toward alcohol or drug use. Seek feedback from outside sources, because the recovering person is locked in a delusional system and can't always see what's really going on in life.

"One of the most important things I've learned about recovery is that if you've been dependent on drugs or alcohol, you cannot safely use these substances," Gorski explains. "The goal needs to be to learn how to live a drug-free life. To do this, you have to learn how to think clearly, logically, and rationally in a sober state. You need to learn how to recognize, label, and communicate your feelings and emotions in a sober state. And you have to learn how to self-regulate your behavior as a sober person. You must readjust from an addiction-centered social life to a sobriety-centered social life."

According to Gorski, addiction has three facets—*biological, psychological* and *social dependence*. People can become dependent on any one of these levels or all three simultaneously. *Biological dependence* refers to a tissue dependency on a drug, which then creates tolerance and withdrawal. With *psychological dependence*, a person has come to rely on drugs or alcohol in order to manage their thinking, feeling, and behaviors. Without these substances, they can't think clearly or deal with feelings. They can't self-regulate their behaviors. *Social dependence* indicates that a person has come to rely on alcohol or drugs to act as a social lubricant or social facilitator; without these, they cannot maintain satisfactory relationships with others.

Does Insurance Pay for Treatment?

Some insurance companies do pay for addiction treatment; however, over the past decade they have become more restrictive for both inpatient and outpatient treatment. The costs for a 28-day inpatient treatment program vary widely, ranging from $14,000 to $30,000. Costs for partial day hospital programs range from $250.00 to $400.00 per day.

Treatment Is Cost Effective

Treating substance abuse not only saves lives, but saves dollars. It is estimated that untreated addiction in the United States costs about $276 billion a year, or an average of $1,050 per person annually. This cost includes such things as medical treatment for injuries, traffic accidents, crime, and days lost in the workplace. Yet, every person in the country could be treated for $45 per year.

A study by the National Institute on Drug Abuse found that each dollar spent on addiction treatment saves $4 to $7 in reduced medical and social costs, and returns $3 in increased worker productivity. The study concluded that each dollar invested in treatment returns $7 to $10 to society.

4

Support for Families

ddiction affects the entire family. All too often, family and friends see the addict as being the only one with "the problem." But, the drug abuser's behavior takes an emotional toll on everyone around him or her. Without insights and understanding, loved ones also spiral deeper into the addiction trap.

If you have an addict in your family, you already know the pain and despair that addiction brings. You already know the shame of it—what will our friends and relatives think of us if they know "Johnny" is an addict? Shame is perhaps one of the most destructive of human emotions, but the emotional turmoil does not end with shame. Living in the midst of addiction produces a range of other painful emotions—confusion, anxiety, and often depression.

Eric's Story

My family suffered for years through my brother's addiction. He was addicted to painkillers. We tried reasoning with him. We pleaded with him. Nothing seemed to work. Still, we tried to do anything we thought might help him. I called more than one doctor to report that my brother was abusing drugs they had prescribed. At one time, my parents and I went to court and tried to have my brother committed for psychiatric help; however, the law required us to prove that he was "crazy," which he was not. We lost the case and infuriated my brother.

Exasperated, we tried to convince my brother to enter a treatment facility voluntarily. He reluctantly agreed to pay a visit to the treatment center with us. Once there, we spoke with a social worker. My brother, who was chemically affected at the time of the visit, was belligerent to say the least. Finally, when we realized he would not agree to entering the rehab program, I recall the social worker telling us, "Go to an Al-Anon meeting. If he won't get help, get help for yourself." I dismissed the suggestion immediately, saying to myself that my brother was the one with the problem—not us.

In hindsight, I realize how much we, too, needed help in understanding addiction. We would have benefited greatly from the support of others who had insights about living with an addict.

Living with Emotional Chaos

Experts describe addiction as causing "insanity," or emotional chaos, within a family. When prescription drugs are involved, this insanity may be intensified. Family members are further confused. At first, they believe their loved one must need the drug. Then, gradually, they question the way the addict is abusing the drugs. Is the doctor aware of this abuse? If so, why does the physician continue to prescribe? Furthermore, these drugs are not coming from a shadowy street dealer—they're being prescribed by health professionals. Even though we know the addict is ultimately responsible, the family questions how a health-care system that heals us and saves lives can be the same system administering a drug that contributes to the destruction of their loved one.

Enabling the Addict

Those of us who have lived with addiction have seen its ravages in the form of family arguments, ruined holidays, legal problems, job loss, financial problems, traffic tickets, and worse—traffic accidents. Indeed, feeling powerless to stop someone you love from destroying himself or herself is an extremely painful experience. Many of us, with only the best of intentions, try to help, try to save our loved one from harm's way. But families, operating out of simple love and concern, often do the wrong thing because they do not understand the dynamics of addiction. Families and friends often enable the addict. Enabling involves rescuing or doing for someone what he or she should be doing himself or herself.

Levels of Enabling

Family and friends enable anytime they try to minimize the consequences of the addict's behavior. There are two stages of enabling—*innocent* and *desperate*.

In the *innocent phase* of enabling, family members think the person is just going through a little difficulty in his or her life, and so they try to "cover up" the consequences. An example of this might be paying the fine for a traffic accident, rather than addressing the underlying cause of the accident. The enabler may say, "Well, this is our beloved Jeff, our beloved Mary, who can't possibly be an addict like those people who live on the other side of the tracks."

In the *desperate phase*, the family finally realizes, because of the continuing consequences, that a loved one has a true addiction problem. They are so horrified that they actually step up the enabling process because they don't want the worst consequences to come about, such as a family member going to jail or losing a job. So they actually go into high gear enabling the problem, paying rent or paying medical expenses that may arise from the addiction.

Jill's Story

My daughter, Laura, was 23 when she began abusing painkillers. The medications had originally been prescribed for legitimate chronic pain, but Laura increased the dosages and began a destructive, five-year bout with addition. We came to realize that we were enabling her.

You can talk until you're blue in the face, but addicts won't get help until they're ready. Most people know, deep down, when they're in trouble—they just won't admit it.

John, 42
In recovery

I used to say my daughter's addiction was like seeing her on a speeding train, heading toward a brick wall, and I could do nothing to stop it. It was so painful to see her destroying herself. In the beginning, we tried to help her, but we really were enabling her. For example, on three separate occasions, we set her up in an apartment. We helped her find each apartment and paid the deposits and first month's rent. We always thought Laura would get on her feet and be responsible. But she didn't. When she didn't pay the rent, the landlords would come looking for us.

Laura was a young woman who never had caused us problems or had been in trouble. But as an addict, she was a different person altogether. We were exasperated. We did have one doctor tell us she was an addict, but we didn't believe it. We knew she needed pain medications, which had been prescribed by a doctor, so we were slow to believe she had an addiction problem.

At one point, Laura's grandmother took her into her home. Laura stole pain pills from her grandfather, who was quite ill at the time. She also caused a lot of damage to the house. She was high on pills and forgot to turn off the water in the bathtub; it overflowed and caused part of the ceiling to collapse. She also stole money from her father and me. One night she ran up a $1,000 dollar phone bill, talking to a "psychic" on a 900 phone line all night. The chaos was ongoing.

Finally, we realized that the more we were helping Laura the more she was failing. We had to quit supporting her. It was very difficult to stop rescuing her, but we did. However, we did not abandon her. We always told her we loved her, and that she could always call us collect, and that we would always be there to help her when she was ready to get help. We have a strong faith in God, and came to believe that only He could show her the way. Fortunately she found the way, and is clean and sober.

Today, my advice for other families is to not rescue or enable the addict in your family. Ask yourself: is what I'm doing helping matters or making them worse? But always let them know you will help them when they're ready to help themselves. Understand that addicts can't recover on their own. It's as if they've fallen into a well with moss-covered sides, and they can't get a grip to pull themselves up. To recover, they must reach out and ask for help. But, until they're ready, always let them know that you love them and that your heart is open.

Detach with Love

So, if it is not constructive to rescue the addict and he or she steadfastly refuses to get into treatment, what can you do? The theory behind the 12-step support programs is to *detach* from the addict. This doesn't mean you stop loving the person. It doesn't mean abandoning the person or not being supportive if he or she decides to get help. It means "detaching in love" and stopping the game of rescue. The Al-Anon literature says "detachment is neither kind nor unkind. It does not imply judgment or condemnation of the person or situation from which we are detaching. It is simply a means that allows us to separate ourselves from the adverse effects that another person's addiction can have upon our lives."

Too often, family and friends become obsessed with rescuing the addict. In the process, we teach addicts that they do not have to face the consequences of their actions—we'll be there to "pick up the pieces." As a result, we become "co-dependents," focused on the lives of the addicts rather than on taking care of ourselves. We succumb to the crises, the chaos, and the heartbreak.

Devon, age 34, spent two years living in the chaos of her husband's addiction to painkillers before she decided to get help for herself. "When my husband went into treatment the third time, I entered a five-day family program. The therapists helped me realize my whole focus was on his life, not mine. I also came to understand that I did not cause his addiction. I cannot control it. I cannot change it. I had to make decisions about what I was going to do about my life, not his. Fortunately today, my husband is in recovery, and I continue to go to Al-Anon meetings. I no longer question him or nag him about whether he's taking pills. We communicate much better and our marriage is strong. I'm sure my getting help has made a difference in his staying sober."

Giving up the role of keeper or rescuer can be difficult, but in the end we family members must come to the realization that all our rescuing has not caused the addict to change. We must learn to take care of ourselves. When family members get the focus back on themselves, the addict often realizes that "game" is ending. Sometimes, he or she may give new consideration to taking responsibility for personal behaviors. Still, don't give up on an addict. Let the individual know that you are ready to help when he or she is ready to get help.

Choosing an Intervention

There are three keys to a successful intervention: plan, plan, plan.

Jeff Jay
Interventionist

In the best case scenario, the addict will decide to seek treatment. But this doesn't always happen. In this case, you may wish to consider an *intervention*. An intervention is a planned event in which the person who is chemically dependent is confronted in an effort to get him or her into treatment immediately. An intervention may be informal or structured.

Informal Intervention

In an *informal intervention*, the individual may be confronted by a family member or friend, or possibly a therapist acting on behalf of the family. Bruce Cotter is a professional interventionist who works with addicts on a one-to-one basis. Having done interventions in which a group confronts an individual, he now prefers to work alone. "People I work with are scared, angry, confused, and paranoid. They're despairing, they're hurting, and they feel guilty. So, I find I can work more effectively with them alone, rather than confronting them with a group."

Cotter cites an example of working with a young man, Robert, from the Midwest. "When I met with the family, I could see how angry they were at their son. I didn't think it would have been good to have them there for the intervention. Instead, I met alone with him at 6:00 o'clock in the morning at a motel. We sat and talked for almost three hours. He told me a lot of things that he wanted to say, that he probably never would have stated in front of his family. Plus, I have credentials as a therapist, but I'm also a recovering addict, so I could assure Robert that I knew what he was going through."

In the course of working with an individual, Cotter wants the addict to *choose* treatment, not be talked into it. "The worst thing you can do is tell an addict what to do. They won't buy it. I want them to make the decision to seek treatment and then I support their decision. They already know they don't want to continue living the way they are, but they are afraid of giving up their drug of choice."

When Cotter is hired to do an intervention, he accompanies an individual to the treatment center. He has all transportation arranged—cars and plane tickets if necessary. He stays with the patient throughout the admission process at the treatment center. Then, a couple of weeks later, Cotter returns to the treatment center to check on the patient and offer his continued support. He also designs an aftercare program of support to be implemented upon the patient's release from a treatment center.

Cotter's services represent one style of informal intervention. If your budget won't cover such extensive involvement, including travel, help is still available. Many therapists and interventionists offer a range of services that may be tailored to fit your needs and budget.

Structured Intervention

A *structured intervention* involves family and friends, and sometimes a counselor. In either case, if the meeting concludes successfully, the individual is driven directly to the waiting treatment facility.

The intervention team is commonly made up of a group of three to eight family members and friends. Each team member needs to make a commitment to learn about the dynamics of addiction and how to intervene properly. This is important since each family member and friend usually has a different idea of what is right. It often helps to have a professional interventionist or therapist help plan and carry out the intervention.

Organizing the Intervention Team

Once assembled, the intervention team can discuss in detail their experiences of the negative consequences with the addict. This is often an eye-opening process because different family members and friends will have had different experiences with the addict; it may be quite a revelation to them to realize how they were involved in enabling. The team should also choose a chairperson and a "detail person," someone who will take care of all the little things about getting ready to get the addict into treatment.

Taking Care of Details

The team members need to plan ways to counter each objection the addict may have about entering treatment. "They need to be prepared for such objections as 'I can't take time off from my job' in which case the family will have already talked to the employer in advance, with the addict's knowledge," according to Jeff Jay, an interventionist and co-author of *Love First: A New Approach to Drug and Alcohol Intervention.*

For someone who lives alone, the objection to going into treatment might be, "Who's going to take care of my dog, Spot?" It's important that the team has excellent answers to these objections. According to Jay, "You will never see an addict who is more shocked than when a team member says to him, 'We know how much your dog Spot likes Uncle Roger, and Roger has agreed to take Spot while you're in treatment. In fact, we're ready to take him over to Roger's house right now.' This kind of preparedness usually causes one's jaw to drop. They're saying to themselves, 'These people have thought of everything! Now is the time for me to get help.' "

Another important matter is to determine what treatment center the person will be going to. Is there insurance or not? The detail person needs to keep track of all this.

Carrying Out the Intervention

When the actual intervention takes place, experts say it's best to have it in a place outside the addict's home. The home of a team member is a good choice. Intervention should be done only when the person is sober, so this often means doing it early in the morning. "It's important to have the most important people of their life there. For example, if it's an adult male, I often try to have his mother walk right up to him, give him a hug, and say, 'Honey, we need to talk.' She may guide him over to the couch and everybody sits down," explains Jay.

He also recommends that the intervention be very tightly scripted, so rather than having people talk off the top of their heads, they actually take turns reading a letter to the addict. "I like to see the letters open up with very loving statements, which is often very surprising to the addict. This is a 180-degree difference from what they're expecting to hear. When the intervention is taking place, the last thing that the addict expects to hear is people telling them what a great person they've been and how important they've been in their life. They expect to be beaten over the head. So what we do is, we put a different twist on it and this kind of destabilizes the addict and gets them ready to hear more."

"For example, a letter to me when I was in my addiction was, 'Dear Jeff: I love you, I care about you, and when I was going through a divorce five years ago, you were the one who was there for me. You're the one I could always count on to speak to, and you gave me such good counsel and support that I couldn't have made it without you. Now I see that you're going through difficulty and I am going to be there for you.' After they tell them how important they've been, their letter can explain, 'I've taken some time to learn about alcoholism and drug addiction, and I understand that you have a medical problem. It's not a character issue. It's not a willpower issue. It's really a medical issue and I want you to get medical help for it.' "

> *Addicts need our help. We often expect them to self-diagnose, which is the one thing they are incapable of doing. They are powerless and paralyzed in their addiction.*
>
> Bruce Cotter
> Interventionist

Next in their letters, the intervention group should move into a "fact reporting" phase in which they list the reasons why the addiction is causing problems. This should include no judgment, no blame, no anger. Just the facts. Then, in closing their letters, each member can reiterate love and concern and ask the addict to get treatment at a very specific treatment center right now. Today.

Joni's Story

Several years ago, I organized an intervention for my brother Jerry, age 40. I felt we had to do something to help him with his addiction. I knew I would always feel bad if we didn't try. I organized a team of ten of us, including family, friends, and colleagues. We prepared for about two months. I read everything I could find about interventions. We also hired a professional interventionist to guide us.

The day we did the intervention, Jerry was invited to a friend's house, where we were all waiting. He was rather shocked to see us all there, especially since several of us had flown in from out of town. But, the second he saw us he knew what was up. He was angry at first, but we'd all been told to expect this, so we did not let his anger dissuade us. We all talked to him, telling him how his addiction had affected him and us; we also stressed how much we loved him and wanted him well.

He tried to make an excuse—that he had to go home and pack. We told him his suitcase had already been packed by his wife; she had brought it over ahead of time. When he insisted that he be able to go home and shower, my other brother went with him. He asked us, "Are you afraid I'll run?" We all said, "Yes." He took a shower, returned, and my other brother and I took him to the treatment center. Four years later, he's still sober.

Looking back, I feel really good about what we did. We helped save his life. So, we had a good outcome, but it wasn't easy. It was a very emotionally taxing experience. It was scary too, because we didn't know if we would succeed.

My advice to others who are considering an intervention: do it. You will always know you tried. I also suggest educating yourself about interventions, read, and be well organized. It's good to have the help of an interventionist or a counselor who understands how interventions are carried out. These professionals can be objective, less emotional, whereas we family members were very emotional and not objective.

Don't Wait for the Problem to Get Better

Remember, addiction is a progressive disease. Without treatment, it gets worse. Too often family members and friends, not understanding the dynamics of addiction, believe the problem will "get better" or that the addict will eventually "get on his feet." An addict's brief period of sobriety may be mistaken for recovery from addiction, when in fact it is only a short reprieve.

Experts suggest working to get help for your loved one now. Don't wait until a more serious health problem arises or until the addict in your family injures himself or others. Take advantage of the many educational opportunities that are available through support groups, treatment centers, and private therapists. The more educated you are, the more you will be prepared to help your loved one.

5

Voices of Hope

All too often, individuals in recovery say they didn't seek treatment early enough or they went to health professionals who didn't understand or diagnose their addiction. Consequently, proper treatment was delayed. Because addiction is an illness that requires first diagnosis and then treatment, it is important that we avail ourselves to those health professionals who understand chemical dependency and how it is treated.

In this chapter, you'll hear from experts on addiction, including addictionologists from the American Society of Addiction Medicine (ASAM), who have treated thousands of individuals for chemical dependency. ASAM is an international association of 3,000 physicians dedicated to improving the treatment of alcoholism and other addictions.

Addiction Is an Illness

Sidney Schnoll, M.D.
Addictionologist

Our culture today treats addicts like we treated epileptics 400 years ago—we burned them at the stake because we thought they were possessed. Now we know these people have a disease that requires specific treatment. I see people who are addicted as suffering from an illness, just as one suffers from diabetes or any other illness. Yet, many see addicts as having something morally wrong with them as if it's something they bring upon themselves.

I became interested in substance abuse and addiction about 30 years ago when I was a resident at Philadelphia General Hospital. I saw a lot of young people coming in with problems from LSD use. No one quite knew how to take care of them.

There is no one treatment for most diseases. And so, there is no one specific treatment for addiction. We're talking about roads to recovery, rather than one road to recovery. There is not one shoe that fits all. I think one of the biggest mistakes made in the field of addiction is that people make the assumption that there's one way to recover and if you don't do it that way there's something wrong with you. For example, not every diabetic needs insulin. And those who get it take different doses. And, diabetics have different courses of progression in their disease. The same is true for addiction. It is a chronic disease just like diabetes. We can treat it, but we cannot cure it. We can control some of the symptoms. We can make some people's lives very comfortable; other people do not do as well.

Anyone who needs help with addiction should seek out the help of someone trained in the diagnosis and assessment of the problems of addiction. Addiction is not something that most physicians are adequately prepared to treat.

,ding on Hope

Clair Bissell, M.D.
Addictionologist

I'm an alcoholic in recovery myself, so I became interested in recovery issues during my own recovery. Some years later I went to medical school and went on to practice addiction medicine full time. My writing and research has dealt almost exclusively with substance abuse and chemical dependency.

If someone who's battling addiction feels hopeless, I would offer them the experience of other people who have recovered, along with the understanding of what the patient is feeling emotionally at the moment. Empathy without sentimentality. Also, if they're feeling really hopeless, I would make a note to myself to see how many suicide attempts there have been. I'd also want to evaluate for depression. If one has come to treatment on his own, he must have a pinch of hope that things might get better, otherwise he wouldn't be there.

When it comes to treating prescription drug addiction, there are some attitudinal differences when comparing it to alcoholism. For example, a good many individuals might think it's naughty to drink, but that it's okay to have certain sedative-hypnotic pills if the doctor has prescribed them. The truth is, these drugs are in the same "family" as alcohol. But pills aren't seen as being as bad as alcohol.

And all too often, these addicts are hard for doctors to spot. They haven't had the training. If the patient comes in with a clean white shirt and clean fingernails—not the stereotype of the drug addict who lives under a bridge—many doctors will not realize the patient is an addict. The diagnosis of addiction is often made by caste and class and is made late rather than early.

If you are an addict or alcoholic in recovery, it's very important to tell your doctor so that you aren't given addictive drugs or cough syrups with alcohol. Doctors need to take a patient's history before prescribing drugs. We need to use these drugs of addiction as little and for as short a time as possible.

Over the years, I saw many patients who were doing quite well in recovery from alcoholism, but went to a physician and were given sedatives or tranquilizers. Then the mood swings began and ultimately they began to drink again. When someone in a case like this takes the sedation and then a couple of drinks they become very relaxed. But in a matter of a few hours, they're going to be more tense than when they started. That's when they're in the rebound, the return of original symptoms which is part of withdrawal. They're having these intense emotional ups and downs. Now, if you're an alcoholic, you already have a body that knows perfectly well what you can do when those up periods feel too uncomfortable—you use more chemicals.

Now, I'm not saying anything whatsoever about the minor use of tranquilizers by people who are not addicts. There's quite a body of information that says these drugs are pretty safe for the occasional user. But for those who have already had problems with alcohol or other drugs, it's a bad idea to start playing with other mood-changing drugs.

I always give this word of warning about drugs of addiction: Whenever you take a drug and it really changes the way you feel, makes you feel really good—be careful. It may be something you should not have.

Let me stress that there are untold thousands who can use drugs wisely. But as a doctor in addiction medicine, I've seen only the casualties on the battlefield over the years. I never saw the patients who took only a few pills and used them wisely. I saw people who got into bad trouble and then came to me for help. I would also say to those recovering from prescription drug addiction, to be patient. It may be a while before they feel a lot better. I saw this especially with benzodiazepines. For example, someone could be clean for two months and still not feel well. It's easy to get discouraged and go back to the pills. They need to hang on—it won't always be as bad.

Finally, I would share some thoughts with families. As part of my work, I also saw many family members who suffered deeply because of a loved one's addiction. When family and friends are trying to cope with an addict, it's important for them to under-stand several things. One, the relative or friend has to realize that they did not cause the problem and they cannot, by themselves, resolve it. Even if the addict is blaming them, they must realize they're not responsible.

Equally important, the relative has got to stop making it easy for the addict to stay sick. The parent who constantly pays the fine or bails his kid out of jail is enabling. The addict does not have to face the consequences of his own behavior.

Another thing that is important for the family to know is what a doctor is going to recommend for the patient, if treatment is underway. For example, the patient might visit a doctor and then go home and tell the family the doctor said it was okay to take a drink or a few drugs once in a while. It helps if the family knows that the physician has recommended total abstinence from alcohol and all other mood-changing drugs of addiction.

Be Cautious with Benzodiazepines

Ronald Gershman, M.D.
Addictionologist

I was a psychiatrist in private practice for twenty years. Most of that time I worked in the treatment of chemical dependency. I treated about 10,000 patients for alcohol and drug problems and detoxed approximately 1,500 patients for benzodiazepines, a strong focus of mine.

When it comes to treating patients, I see two patterns. First, there is essentially the drug addict who supports an addiction through the use of prescription pills. They see themselves as different from other addicts; they often think their prescribed medication is justified even though they may be manipulating and deceptive in acquiring excessive amounts of drugs. Second, I see the individuals we call the "unwitting" or "iatrogenic" addicts. These patients were put on medication (especially benzodiazepines) for legitimate reasons, but for an extended period of time and became addicted.

How do such addictions occur? Benzodiazepines aside for a moment, let's look at opiates, which are commonly used to treat pain. When people take an opiate medication, the drug relieves physical pain and it also relieves emotional pain. The problem of abuse comes in using the drug to relieve emotional pain.

For most patients, if they're using the drug strictly to relieve physical pain, when the physical pain is gone, they can give up the drug. But if they're depressed or anxious or life is miserable for them, then the drug use can become a problem after the physical pain is eliminated. The emotional pain is still there and they still want to treat that pain. From what I've seen, this is a pretty clear pattern, but it's not easy to tell which patients might end up seeking the drug for emotional pain once they've healed physically.

The treatment for addiction differs dramatically, depending on the nature of the drug you're treating. For example, treatment for a benzodiazepine addiction is very different from treatment for an opiate such as Vicodin or codeine.

Managing the withdrawal and keeping the patient from relapsing is the real crux of the problem. The detox for the opiates is about seven to ten days and can usually be done on an outpatient basis. I used about eight different medications to help patients get through the detox. Among the medications we used was an opiate blocker, which prevented an opiate from "working" if the patient relapsed. We also used antidepressants because the depressions are quite severe and are a major cause of relapse. Then, with therapy, we helped the patient learn to live and manage a sober life, which is really the heart and soul of the work that needs to be done. This detox is usually quite successful if the patient is highly motivated.

But the detox for benzodiazepines is more difficult. It takes longer, ranging perhaps from six to eighteen months. In this recovery, the ongoing, relentless withdrawals can be incapacitating. The "fallout" from addiction to these drugs can lead to the breakup of marriages, the loss of businesses, and hospitalizations. Unfortunately, suicide is probably the single most serious side effect.

All too often, this withdrawal pattern is not recognized by doctors. The patient has been on the drugs for a year or so and then the doctor says, "I don't think you need these anymore," and takes them off. In a few days, when the patient breaks down, the doctor and patient assume the "old psychiatric problem" is returning. The patient is hospitalized and put on drugs. This cycle can prevent getting to the root of the dependency problem.

If benzodiazepines are used inappropriately and the patient becomes addicted, the patient builds tolerance and the drugs stop working. In fact, over a long period of time, their usage can worsen the condition they were being used to treat. What happens is, the level of the drug in the blood drops between doses, which quickly brings on withdrawal symptoms. So the drug is losing its effectiveness while the withdrawal is making symptoms three or four times worse than they were before.

I believe benzodiazepines are appropriate for short-term management of acute anxiety or panic attack. Short-term use generally means two weeks to six weeks, the absolute maximum.

Using Benzodiazepines Responsibly

David Mee-Lee, M.D.
Addictionologist

There is disagreement in the medical community about the use of benzodiazepines. Although some say benzodiazepines are overused, some would say the opposite, that they're being underutilized out of doctors' concerns that patients will become addicted.

Opinions vary, even by country. Britain has been very strict in limiting use of benzodiazepines to shorter-term use. In the United States, the fear of abuse has been overblown and patients are being robbed of adequate use because of fear of addiction.

My view is that these drugs are like alcohol, in that not everyone is going to use them inappropriately. I think long-term use can be acceptable as long as the risks and benefits are weighed cautiously and careful assessment of the patient is done to make sure those at high risk for addiction are screened out.

Even if a patient is not at high risk for addiction, the physician should always periodically reassess the use of any medication to see if the patient still needs it. I don't believe drugs should be prescribed blindly just because the patient is not becoming addicted. There are other ways to cope.

Of course, anyone taking even therapeutic doses of a benzodiazepine for a period of time will become tolerant of the drug and will have to be gradually withdrawn from it. To quit abruptly

Stages of Chemical Dependency

Stage	Description
Abstinence	Person has not begun to use the drug, but attitudes are developing
Non-problem use	No negative consequences of use
High-risk use	Use is frequent, heavy, or usage patterns are dangerous
Problem use (or abuse)	First negative consequences arise from usage patterns
Chemical dependence: Early stage	Reversible, less serious negative consequences of threats do not motivate corrective adjustment of usage patterns
Chemical dependence: Middle stage	Irreversible negative consequences of use do not motivate significant corrective adjustment of usage patterns
Chemical dependence: Late stage	Multiple, serious, irreversible negative consequences have failed to motivate corrective adjustment of usage patterns

From "Finding Substance Abusers" by M.P. Liepman et al., 1984. *Family Medicine Curriculum Guide to Substance Abuse.* (Society for Teachers of Family Medicine, Kansas City, Missouri) Reprinted by permission.

would cause withdrawal. But not everyone would have to be detoxed on an inpatient basis.

The people who often get in trouble are those who have escalated their use of the drug; they take high dosages and are often in a poor recovery environment. They may also lack emotional support and have poor impulse control in terms of relapse. Most people will do better if they have motivation to come off the drug and have more resources, both personal and environmental, to help them deal with impulsive use.

We need to understand a couple of basics about addiction. One, addiction affects not only the person using, but those around—family and friends. There are very few families who aren't affected by addiction in some way. Also, the one who has the problem needs to acknowledge that there is a problem. Family members and others can be helpful by confronting and not rescuing the person.

The patients who obtain pharmaceuticals through legal means, but escalate dosages and abuse the drugs, often have trouble admitting to their problem. They tend to say they were just doing what their doctors told them. They don't see themselves as addicts. We try to help these patients see that their drug use has been negatively affecting their lives. Some of these patients come to treatment once their doctor has judged they've become addicted and has stopped prescribing. The patients are sometimes left not knowing what to do if they're not guided into treatment.

What goes into successful recovery? Anyone can succeed. The degree of difficulty depends on how much damage has already been done. Has the patient lost jobs, family, and physical health? The more one has lost, the harder recovery might be.

Recovery from addiction is similar to recovering from other chronic illnesses. You have to keep monitoring it to make sure you're taking care of yourself. It means continuing in some kind of recovery program. That doesn't mean going to support groups daily for the rest of your life, but rather continuing to be vigilant about relapse and using support groups or other methods to stay aware.

Some people can recover on their own. They come to the awareness that they have a problem and decide to do something about it. Not everyone goes through treatment. Many people can do something about it themselves. Others need help.

And, in the scenario in which the addict won't get into recovery, his or her family can still recover. They can learn to stop playing into the addict's agenda and learn to stop passing the problem on down through generation after generation.

In short, people with chemical dependencies must first remember that they have an illness; second, realize they're at risk for relapse; and third, recognize that they need ways to cope with stress or problems if they're heading toward relapse. Addiction is a chronic illness, not a moral problem. It needs treatment, not judgment.

Addiction to Pills Creates More Denial

Patrick Dalton
Certified Addiction Counselor

On a scale of 1 to 10, how serious is prescription drug abuse in the United States? I would say a 10. The individuals we see are outpatients. Many are addicted to prescription drugs. We insist that they divulge all information about the drugs they are taking in order for us to treat them effectively. Often, they're getting drugs from doctors who aren't aware of addiction issues. The doctor might be trying to eliminate a patient's pain but not understand potential addiction problems. If the patient is prone to addiction, this can be like feeding gasoline to a fire.

Those dependent on prescription drugs have a mind-set different from that of alcoholics. Most of the people I've treated are very resistant to letting go of their drugs. They can partially justify it because they've gotten their drugs legitimately, from a doctor. (They don't have the stigma of being a user of street drugs.) This causes a high degree of relapse. In addition to this denial, those who are prescription-drug dependent have a real fear of not being able to cope without their drugs. They are very "med-seeking," always wanting a pill to fix them.

Some people don't realize they are prone to addiction, and they get hooked on a legal drug. They may not realize it until they start having negative consequences in their lives. When you use a chemical of any kind, once it's brought negative consequences to your life, you're crossing the line into addiction. Anyone who is aware of his or her addictive tendencies should always tell a treating physician.

Realizing Risk for Addiction

Sheila Blume, M.D.
Addictionologist

Not everyone who takes painkillers or sedatives gets addicted, but anyone who does take them should be warned of their addictive potential. In my experience, those who become addicted to these drugs fall into several categories.

The most common is the person who is an alcoholic but doesn't know it—the alcoholism hasn't been diagnosed and the person is being seen for associated symptoms such as insomnia, tension, difficulty concentrating. Then, an addictive drug is prescribed and the patient becomes addicted.

Equally unfortunate is the patient who has recovered from alcoholism but does not understand the potential of other drugs and becomes addicted to them. These people may have recovered from earlier addictions on their own, without treatment or self-help groups. Many, many people do this. However, if they haven't been in a treatment program, they may not have been educated about other mood-altering drugs. This knowledge could have saved many self-recovering people from additional trouble.

Family members need to get help for themselves. They think the addict is the only one with the problem. But when they don't get help, some families literally love the addict to death.

Sharon Hartman
Caron Foundation

I recall the case of one man, a recovering alcoholic, who had separated his shoulder. Because he had stopped using alcohol on his own, he really didn't see himself as an alcoholic. So, when he was given Tylenol with Codeine for pain, he got hooked on it and, in the end, it almost killed him.

All recovering addicts need to tell any doctor, including dentists, that they should not be given habit-forming drugs. If a doctor tells a recovering patient that the drugs won't cause dependency problems, but the patient still isn't sure, he should check with the pharmacist about any such dangers with the drug.

Another category of people who are susceptible to dependence are those in a lot of emotional distress or agitation. Once prescribed a sedative or tranquilizer, they can become dependent. For people who have not been drug dependent before, the first symptom of dependence is that the drug becomes very precious to them. They always make sure they have it with them at all times. They have the prescription refilled well in advance so they won't run out. They think it's the most wonderful thing in the world, and it helps them.

Then, when they hit a point where something bothers them emotionally, they take more of the drug and that feels good. Then, they begin to increase the dose. At this point, they may get wary and decide not to tell their doctor about how they're using the drug. They fear their doctor won't approve and will stop prescribing. They begin to justify their use of the drug through denial or rationalization. They might start to manipulate the doctor, saying they lost a prescription or they're going on a trip and need extra pills. This works for only a short time, so then they'll have to switch to another doctor. They may have five or six doctors they can reliably go to. They know exactly what drug they want when they schedule an appointment.

There is a point when abuse becomes addiction. Abuse refers to dangerous use, like taking a drug and driving when you should not be driving under the influence of the drug. And often people can stop at abuse, but if they don't they move on to dependence.

My message of hope is that prescription drug addiction is a treatable disease. Sometimes it's harder to do an intervention with prescription drugs than with alcohol or illegal drugs. Patients often believe they really don't need treatment. But treatment can help them return to a productive life. Recovery is very possible

Addicts Are Not Having Fun

Howard Heit, M.D.
Addictionologist / Pain Specialist

When a person who needs treatment is reluctant to get help, I ask, "Are you having a good time?" The patient is usually taken aback by that because even though the public perceives that addicts are having a good time, the addict knows deep down that he or she is *not* having a good time. I remind them that they're not. Why aren't they? First, they wake up each day worrying about their supply of pills, whether they're going to be able to "work" doctors for more drugs, or get drugs illicitly, which is very expensive. Second, they have a poor quality of life, given their drug-seeking behavior. So, if they're not having a good time, and their habit is expensive, degrading, and scary, I ask, "Why not try a program of recovery?" Most people will eventually agree.

I explain the kinds of changes that they have to make to stay in recovery. And, very early when they're having some difficulties making changes, I give them this homework assignment.

"Do you have a pen with you?" I ask.

"No," they'll say.

"Here's an official pharmaceutical pen. Do you have a pad with you?"

"No, I don't."

"Here's an official pharmaceutical pad you can keep. Now, how long does it take you to get home?"

"Half an hour," they may say.

"I want you to take an hour, to take a long way home. And on your way home, I want you to count the number of dinosaurs that you see."

This causes them to stop and ponder my suggestion. "I'm not going to see any dinosaurs."

"Exactly," I respond. "The dinosaurs didn't adapt. They didn't survive. And now you have to make these adaptations or changes in your life if you want to stay on Earth. I will help you, but it takes work."

If they choose to work with me, I first take a very thorough medical history. The overwhelming majority of times, these are good people, solid people, intelligent. But, in their history I might find such things as a sleep disorder, depression, a psychiatric problem that has gone undiagnosed and untreated. These underlying causes are partly to blame for them using the drugs excessively and becoming addicted. I validate what has happened to them and again explain why their body has become used to or physically dependent on these medicines.

I advise families to go to an addiction therapist and tell their story. Find out what they can do to help a loved one and realize how serious this disease of addiction is.

James Mulligan, M.D

Consider the benzodiazepine Xanax, for example. I explain to a patient that I can safely wean him or her off Xanax by switching to a long-acting benzodiazepine. I point out that a short-acting benzodiazepine like Xanax has what we call an "off-and-on switch." That is, the level of Xanax in the blood fluctuates off and on, up and down, giving one the positive reinforcement, the craving, and the alteration of the biological and physiological system. These cravings kick in like clockwork with short-acting benzos, and the majority of the drugs of abuse are short-acting. I explain that I'm going to switch them to another drug in the same class that will go to the same receptor site on the brain, but it's a long-acting medication. Therefore, instead of falling off and on the receptor site, it will stay there for a twenty-four hour period. Then what I do is slowly reduce the dose so that the brain gets used to slow reduction of the drug, and we "wean" them off the medication. We never want to stop the benzo abruptly, since doing so can cause seizures.

I may further explain that I have also noted in their medical history a sleep disorder or other emotional problem. "Gee, it sounds like you have anxiety or are depressed. While we're working on this, let me place you on another medication—one that is non-addictive—to help you with the sleep problem."

Here, I also stress the importance of changing behaviors. In the past, this patient conditioned himself or herself to reach for a pill when life becomes stressful. I introduce them to what I call a "Thoughts, Feelings, Actions, and Alternatives Diary." I ask them to record what happens when they feel the need to take a pill. They may write, "I want to take a Xanax. Why do I want to take a Xanax? I'm sad. My action is to take a Xanax. Wait a minute. What is my alternative? Maybe I will go and speak to my significant other and resolve this difficulty that we're having."

As another part of the treatment, I may also bring in a trained therapist to work on identifying and handling the "trigger points"—those stressors that make them want to use the drug. And so the recovery process is underway.

In short, the process works like this. You have the powerful primitive part of the brain that likes the feelings drugs bring; I call this part the "dark angel." And, you have the "white angel," the intellectual part of the brain that handles thoughts, feelings, and actions. The task is to bring in the white angel to handle the dysfunctional trigger points that lead to destructive behaviors.

Warning Signs of Addiction

David Gastfriend, M.D.
Addictionologist

I would say about 15 percent of our practice involves prescription drug dependence. We see a range of patients.

At one end of the range are patients who have been prescribed a drug from the Valium family, like Xanax, for treatment of panic disorder. Initially they got relief from the drug, but then needed increased doses to achieve their state of comfort. Then they have difficulty coming off the medication, even though they want to discontinue it. This is a case of physiological dependence, not addiction, and it's very common with these medications even when they are used correctly and safely. Treatment is a matter of tapering the doses, educating the patient about what to expect, and teaching the patient to use behavioral techniques to cope with modest withdrawal symptoms. This is the most common problem we see.

> *I tell patients they don't have to live in emotional pain. They believe their pills are the only way to cope with the pain, but they come to realize they don't have to live that way. Help is available.*
>
> Bruce Cotter
> Interventionist

At the other end of the range are those who are fully dependent on either alcohol, cocaine, or narcotics and are compulsively seeking to get high. They will use prescription drugs in combination with illegal drugs. Or, when they can't get heroin, they'll substitute with prescription opiates or benzodiazepines. They are truly addicted, manipulative, and compelled by their disease to beat the system. Often they feign illness to multiple doctors. These patients make up a smaller element of the overall problem, but it's a very costly problem in terms of death, emergency room visits, thefts, auto accidents, firearm accidents, and drug trading.

The mid-range of patients that I see are those who have been prescribed medications and who have psychological problems, although these problems initially may not have been apparent. Such problems include dependency on others, impulsiveness under stress, and paranoia. For these patients, certain drugs can create physiological and psychological dependence. This begins the cycle of addiction—compulsive use—resulting in an urge to use the substance at high personal costs.

We know there are individuals who are highly vulnerable to becoming alcoholic for genetic reasons, but we don't have reliable research on genetic vulnerability to addiction to anxiety medications and prescription narcotics. But, there is work developing that infers that the same genetic vulnerability exists. Many drugs have the same physiological effects as alcohol.

Patients in this category are often referred to us addiction specialists once their doctors realize they're being manipulated into prescribing excessive doses. The doctor may not want to cut off the patient completely from the drug and will call for a consultation with an addiction specialist.

There are warning signs that indicate prescription drug use is becoming problematic. Addiction problems could be arising when:

- You start to feel that the drug, at the same dose, isn't working as well as it used to.
- You feel the drug wearing off before it's time to take the next dose.
- You experience more than symptom relief as the drug takes effect; there is some degree of excitement or high.

This indicates the dose may be excessive or that the medication may work too rapidly for safe, long-term use.

- You feel subdued or lethargic within a few hours of taking the medication. This may be an another indication that the dose is excessive.

- You're irritable and have problems sleeping. Here, the medication may be too short-acting and may produce mild withdrawal over the course of the sleep cycle.

- You feel that you can perform certain tasks or engage in certain activities (like driving through traffic or socializing at a party) only with the benefit of the medication. This feeling increases with time.

If you note any of these warning signs, you should speak to your physician. Consider a consultation with an addiction specialist. Also, review your past history and your family history for substance use. Did your parents, grandparents, or siblings have problems with medications or substances like alcohol?

If a patient has run into problems with a drug, we expect them to take some responsibility for their behavior and ask for help. Many are afraid to ask questions for fear they'll be cut off from the drug and they'll suffer. But in order to reasonably and ethically prescribe some of these medications, the physician counts on the patient to be a partner in fostering good health.

Support Groups Help Avoid Isolation

Jeff Baldwin, Pharm.D.
Associate Professor of Pharmacy

It's important to recognize that there's not a specific level of drug or alcohol use that determines when you're addicted. For example, I've seen a woman who was alcoholic on one beer a day, and I've seen a man who was alcoholic on a case of beer a day. The better definition of addiction is "continuing to use a substance once it brings negative consequences to your life."

Once we do have an addiction, I believe one of the most important things for recovering is faithfully going to meetings, 12-step or support groups. And, recovering people who first go to 12-step groups also should understand that they may need to be on some medications during their recovery. Many attending those meetings mean well, but will say that if you're taking any drug that has mood-altering properties, you are not "clean." I do not agree with these individuals. In fact, some 40 percent of alcoholics and addicts have a dual diagnosis, meaning they have other clinically apparent psychiatric illnesses (such as manic-depression) that require medication. Other people might need antidepressants to help lift them from depression and help stop the demons screaming inside their heads.

Further, it may help those who have gotten off addictive drugs to understand that, at some point in their lives, they may have to take controlled substance drugs for medical reasons (such as for pain after surgery). This is not a death sentence, but needs to be treated carefully by the health professional and the patient. The patient should be given no more of the drug than is absolutely necessary. And, probably the best thing to do is to treat the experience as if it were a relapse. Assume that the patient will lose control of the decision to use or not to use the drug excessively. In other words, it's a controlled relapse, not a drug-seeking behavior.

Also, if you have a dependency, find a physician who understands addiction. You also need a pharmacist who understands addiction. For example, if you need an over-the-counter cold preparation, the pharmacist can help you choose one that is safer for you.

We need to remember, too, that once someone has been addicted, they're not immune from becoming addicted to other substances. This includes alcohol, even if they've never been alcoholic. It's often tough for people to accept that alcohol is risky. But once they've been addicted to a mood-altering substance and they have the brain chemistry that predisposes them to dependency, they're at risk.

The use of alcohol can lead to drug relapse. Alcohol can lower their inhibitions and they may decide to "use" again. It's also common to switch addictions from pills to alcohol, or vice versa.

Recovering individuals also should know about relapse counseling. This involves teaching the recovering person to recognize the early warning signals of impending relapse. Relapse is not just picking up a pill all of a sudden and taking it. Relapse is a long path of events; individuals can usually identify the sorts of things that lead them in a downhill spiral toward relapse. For example, someone might start feeling anxious and start acting it out sexually, spending money, or being nasty with people. These may be warning signs that they need to get back to support meetings and talk to people. They're starting to isolate, which is a setup for relapse.

6

Pain Management & Fear of Addiction

It is estimated that 20 percent of Americans suffer from chronic pain. Nearly three-quarters of this group report that pain interferes with daily activities, and about two-thirds of those with chronic pain take pain medication daily. The major causes of pain, other than cancer, are headaches, back pain, and arthritis. Many causes of pain are related to aging, and most chronic pain sufferers are middle-aged or older. From 1990 to 1998, the use of painkillers increased 181 percent.

Still, much pain is undertreated. Federal guidelines estimate that as many as half of the 13 million people who have surgery annually receive inadequate pain management. It's also estimated that as many as 80 percent of cancer patients do not receive adequate medication for pain.

Why Is Pain Undertreated?

Fear of Addiction

One of the main barriers to effective pain management is fear of addiction—by both patients and health professionals. "In the past few years we've tried to focus on improving pain management because we know that for the past several decades pain has not been well controlled," according to Betty R. Ferrell, R.N., Ph.D., associate research scientist on pain management, City of Hope National Medical Center, Duarte, California. "When we talk to cancer patients about pain control, they are afraid they'll become drug addicts."

According to Ferrell, even terminally ill patients fear addiction. "Some cancer patients who need serious pain management are often afraid of becoming 'junkies.' We've had parents whose children are dying with cancer say, 'My son is not going to die a junkie, so he should not have that pain medication.' Children have had to talk parents into giving them their medication. In these cases, we explain the difference between drug addiction and physiological dependence. In the latter case, if the patient should eventually come off the pain medication, it would be done gradually with medical supervision; otherwise, the patient would have withdrawal."

High-profile cases also create myths about addiction, explains Ferrell. "When we hear about a celebrity who's addicted to prescription drugs, we think we're all candidates for such addiction; however, these celebrities usually have a history of alcoholism or addiction. And it is those patients who do have a history of substance abuse who can become addicted to their medication."

Under-Education of Physicians

Studies indicate that medical students and residents lack pain management training. In one study, reported by the *Journal of the American Board of Family Practice,* 88 percent of the doctors stated that their training in pain management was poor.

Seventy-three percent stated their residency training was fair or poor.

To avoid problems with addiction, pain management experts stress the importance of proper evaluation of patients; such evaluation may determine whether a patient has underlying emotional problems (such as depression or anxiety) that may predispose them to escalating doses and becoming addicted. Experts also stress the importance of continued re-evaluation of patients to detect signs of addiction.

Doctors' Concerns About Being Investigated

Creating public awareness about the abuse of prescription drugs, especially painkillers, creates serious concern for health professionals who deal in pain management. Media coverage about the abuse of painkillers may cause doctors to decrease the amount of painkillers they prescribe. They often have concerns that they may come under scrutiny and their medical licenses may be at risk if they appear to be prescribing too many controlled substances, even though some patients may need ongoing, high dosages of painkillers to combat pain.

"Reluctance to prescribe opioids for intractable pain can often be attributed to physicians' perceptions that they will be investigated for violation of laws governing controlled substances," according to David Joranson, Associate Director for Policy Studies with the Pain Research Group at the University of Wisconsin. "These laws and regulations amount to legal barriers to pain management. The medical use of controlled substances can provide great improvements in the quality of life for millions of people with debilitating medical conditions."

Joranson acknowledges the need for diversion control; however, he also stresses the importance of not restricting legitimate patients' access to narcotics for pain. "It is essential that we evaluate the barriers to effective pain relief. It's important to understand that opioid analgesics are the mainstay in the treatment of acute pain. Consumers should talk to caregivers if pain is not being treated sufficiently."

Barriers to Effective Pain Management

Problems Related to Patients
- Reluctance to report pain
- Concern about distracting physicians from treatment of the underlying disease
- Fear that pain means disease is worse
- Concern about not being a "good" patient
- Reluctance to take pain medications
- Fear of addiction or being thought of as an addict
- Worries about unmanageable side effects
- Concern about becoming tolerant to pain medications

Problems Related to Health Professionals
- Inadequate knowledge of pain management
- Poor assessment of pain
- Concern about regulation of controlled substances
- Fear of patient addiction
- Concern about side effects of analgesics
- Concern about patients becoming tolerant to analgesics
- Problems related to the Health-Care System

- Low priority given to cancer pain treatment
- Inadequate reimbursement
- Restrictive regulation of controlled substances
- Availability of treatment or access to treatment

Risk of Addiction from Pain Treatment

Studies confirm that the incidence of addiction is low among patients who are treated for legitimate pain, who use pain medications as directed, and who are evaluated regularly. According to the National Institute on Drug Abuse, in a study of 12,000 patients who were given opioids for acute pain, only 4 became addicted. And, even long-term use of pain medications shows a limited risk of addiction. In another study of 38 chronic pain patients, who received opioids for four to seven years, only 4 became truly addicted.

Low Risk for Cancer-Related Pain

"Indeed, the risk of addiction to opioid drugs from legitimate pain management is low," according to Russell K. Portenoy, M.D., chair of the Department of Pain Medicine and Palliative Care at Beth Israel Medical Center in New York City and noted authority on pain management and addiction. "There is a very large clinical experience with chronic cancer-related pain, treated in hospitals and outpatient settings, which suggests that addiction is rare. I've been treating cancer patients full-time for about fifteen years and I have seen a true addiction only a couple of times," says Portenoy.

Higher Risk for Chronic, Nonmalignant Pain

On the other hand, Portenoy suggests that patients being treated as outpatients for chronic, nonmalignant pain have a higher rate of addiction. "If I were to estimate, I would say that somewhere between 5 and 6 percent of the patients with chronic, nonmalignant pain who are referred to pain centers are truly addicted and have shown drug-seeking behavior."

How do valid pain patients get themselves into trouble with pain medications? This may occur if patients are not honest with themselves and their physician. For example, a problem with addiction may arise if a patient's chronic pain still exists, but he or she starts using opioids to treat new or pre-existing problems with anxiety, depression, sleep disorders, or adverse social or economic problems.

If informed that these other, under-lying problems may be cropping up, the physician can treat them accordingly. For example, the patient may need help with coping skills and can be referred to a therapist. Or, the patient may need other (non-opioid) medications. In the case of depression, antidepressants would be the preferred medication rather than having the patient take increased doses of opioids.

> *OxyContin is an excellent pain medication. My patients like it better than morphine, because of the time release. It's unfortunate that it has found its way into the hands of abusers.*
>
> —Cliff Bernstein, M.D.
> Waismann Institute

Seek Pain Specialists

The advice for any patient with severe chronic pain: seek out health professionals with a pain management subspecialty. Neurologists, physiologists, psychiatrists, nurses, and other specialists are well trained in pain management. The expertise of these specialists will usually exceed that of your primary care physician.

Treating chronic, nonmalignant pain is complicated because the needs of those who suffer with it are diverse. For example, the most common nonmalignant pain is arthritis pain, which requires a specific treatment. The most common pains presented to pain specialists are lower back pain and headache, which may require different courses of treatment. Other patients have medical disorders such as shingles, diabetic neuropathy, sickle-cell disease, and hemophilia. Portenoy describes the therapies for some of these patients as "excellent," with high success rates. For other groups the therapies are "hit-and-miss," and the success rates are not predictable.

Pain Is Treatable

The most important thing for consumers to know: pain relief is available for large numbers of patients. Widely accepted medical treatment for cancer pain shows a success rate of 70 to 90 percent, if a patient's physician follows a standard, accepted guideline for pain control. Similarly, if appropriate guidelines are followed for the treatment of acute pain, such as postoperative pain in hospital settings, the success rate for treatment is 90 to 95 percent. If patients have any concern at all that they're losing control and becoming addicted, they need to be honest about this with their physician and get an evaluation by someone who can make a proper diagnosis.

7

Seniors: At Risk for Drug Misuse and Addiction

The incidence of drug abuse among seniors is, in part, a result of their exposure to multiple drugs. People 65 and older make up 13 percent of the U.S. population, yet they take 30 percent of all prescription drugs sold in the United States. It is not unusual for a senior patient to be taking ten to fifteen medications a year, five of them simultaneously at any given time. And, seniors may be seeing multiple physicians, getting different medications from each doctor, but not reporting it.

Each year, drug misuse among seniors accounts for more than 9 million adverse drug reactions and 245,000 hospitalizations. Twenty-five percent of nursing home admissions occur annually as a result of seniors' inability to use medicines safely.

Adverse Drug Interactions

If care is not taken to see that drugs work safely together, the results can be harmful. Seniors are more prone to adverse drug reactions because they metabolize drugs differently than younger individuals. As we grow older, normal changes in the body result in a decrease in the percentage of water and lean tissue and an increase in fat. Also, the kidneys and liver can begin to function less efficiently. Both these factors affect the time a drug stays in the body and the amount absorbed by body tissues.

Medications Potentially Harmful to Seniors

In the first national study of its kind, researchers at Harvard University reported in 1994 that 28 percent of the nation's senior citizens—nearly 7 million people—are taking prescribed drugs considered dangerous to their health. Experts say the study only scratches the surface, that one-half to two-thirds of senior citizens living in communities are being prescribed drugs that are doing unnecessary harm to them. These drugs range from those that may cause dizziness to those that may increase the risk of bone marrow toxicity and cause dangerous fluid retention. (See drug list on page 115.)

Sedatives

What is the biggest risk factor for seniors in taking medications? "Taking sedatives or sleeping pills is the most dangerous thing for elderly people," says Dr. Steffie Woolhandler, co-author of the Harvard study. "The drugs don't wear off by morning, leaving senior citizens sleepy and confused and prone to falling and hip fractures."

Woolhandler, a former professor at Harvard Medical School, attributes part of the problem of seniors taking potentially harmful drugs to physicians "misprescribing." "The education for young physicians about drug use is abysmal. We do not do a very good job teaching medical students about drug therapy. Medical educators need to do a better job of teaching physicians about medications."

Statistics from nursing homes on the use of tranquilizers are also cause for concern. According to one study, published in 1987 by the *New England Journal of Medicine,* 14 percent of hip fractures are attributed to the adverse effects of tranquilizers or painkillers. If you have a relative in a nursing home, ask the staff once or twice a year for a medical review of all drugs being prescribed.

Addiction Among Seniors

Approximately 17 percent of those 60 and older are affected by prescription drug abuse. Approximately 11 percent of women over the age of 59 are addicted to psychoactive prescription drugs, according to Columbia's National Center on Addiction and Substance Abuse. As part of its study on drug abuse in senior women, the center reviewed prescriptions for 13,000 mature women over a six-month period. The report concluded that half of the prescriptions for tranquilizers and sleeping pills should not have been given or should have been given for a shorter period of time.

Recognizing Addiction in Seniors

Addiction in seniors is usually less recognizable than that in younger individuals. Seniors often live alone, so family and friends may not notice the telltale signs of addiction. Seniors are often retired, so work-related problems don't show up; nor do they seem to get as many traffic citations for driving under the influence.

Symptoms of addiction in seniors may include memory loss, depression, mood swings, irritability, inability to concentrate, and talk of suicide. Friends and relatives may view these symptoms as being part of aging and the losses that usually accompany getting older.

Unfortunately, physicians are often not experienced in diagnosing addiction in seniors. As part of the Columbia study on addiction in seniors, 400 doctors were asked to give their top five diagnoses in a hypothetical case in which a patient exhibited the symptoms of early-stage alcoholism. Less than 1 percent of the doctors mentioned alcoholism as a diagnosis. Ninety-three percent of the physicians listed depression as their top diagnosis.

Alcohol and Drug Combinations Increase Risks

Also, an estimated 10 percent of seniors drink heavily—twelve to twenty-one drinks per week; they are poor at reporting alcohol use, often because they are ashamed of it. For example, when a 62-year-old California woman fell and broke her hip, the hospital staff was unaware that she had been taking Valium, drinking wine, and had become chemically dependent. The combination of chemicals caused her fall. "On the fourth day after her hip surgery, she started having very serious withdrawal symptoms," says Dr. David Smith, former president of the American Society of Addiction Medicine. "It's a substantial problem in the elderly. Fifty percent of delirium in the elderly in hospitals is related to the side effects of prescription drugs." Confusion, slurred speech, and memory loss are also side effects.

Getting Treatment

Since substance abuse among seniors is grossly under-diagnosed, only a small percentage are referred to treatment. Other barriers to treatment are pessimism, shame, and denial. The senior and his or her family may fail to acknowledge the problem.

And, if the problem is acknowledged, elderly persons may question the value of getting sober at a time when they may believe they have only have a few years left to live.

Finally, like many others, senior citizens often view addiction as a moral problem rather than as an illness to be diagnosed and treated. "Seniors are especially sensitive about this, and this attitude presents an obstacle to getting treatment," according to Carol Colleran, Director of Older Adult Services at the Hanley Hazelden Foundation, a nationally recognized addiction treatment facility. "Seniors are usually very ashamed of their addiction problem and often quite angry about needing help."

Accordingly, it's important that family members be supportive and help seniors understand that chemical dependency is an illness. "If you have diabetes, you take insulin. If you have high cholesterol, you take cholesterol-lowering medications," explains Colleran. "If you have an addiction, you need to get treatment for it, too." Colleran offers the following advice for family members dealing with seniors who may have become chemically dependent:

- Don't try to reason with a person while he or she is under the influence of a drug.
- Avoid harsh confrontation. Be gentle in discussing problems.
- Avoid use of the word "drug addict," since this term carries a heavy stigma among seniors.
- Understand that throwing away pills won't help. An individual who is not ready to receive help will only replenish the supply.
- Be direct and be specific about your concerns for the individual. Let the person know your family is concerned

about his or her well-being and that he or she is loved and cared for.

Will Insurance Pay for Treatment?

Funding for addiction treatment is likely not covered by insurance. In many cases, insurance companies or Medicare will pay for inpatient detox, which is considered a medical procedure; and Medicare will pay for medical costs for addiction-related injuries such as falls. However, Medicare does not usually pay for primary treatment for addiction.

On a positive note, seniors, overall, are more likely to complete treatment programs, once they enter them. Those who become chemically dependent late in life show the best response to treatment.

Avoiding Drug Misuse and Addiction

Brown Bag Days

What can you do to prevent dangerous drug misuse by an elderly person? Participate in a "brown bag day." At least once a year, put all medications in a brown bag and take them to a doctor or pharmacist and ask for an evaluation, or *medicine review*. The process should be repeated whenever a new drug is added. If you have access to the Internet, you may wish to check drug regimens for potential interactions with each other by typing in your list of drugs at www.drugchecker.drkoop.com, a site set up by Dr. C. Everett Koop, the former U.S. surgeon general. Still, it's recommended that you also discuss drug regimens with your pharmacist and physician.

Among the common problems discovered during medicine reviews:

Drugs to Avoid if You're Over 65

Tranquilizers, Sleeping Aids

Diazepam *(Valium)*. tranquilizer. Addictive, too long-acting.

Chlordiazepoxide *(Librium, Librax)*. tranquilizer. Causes falls.

Flurazepam *(Dalmane)*. sleeping aid. May cause falls.

Meprobamate *(Miltown, Equagesic, Equanil)*. tranquilizer. May cause falls.

Pentobarbitol *(Nembutal)*. sedative. Addictive.

Secobarbitol (Seconal). sedative. Addictive.

Antidepressants

Amitriptyline *(Elavil, Endep, Etrafon, Limbitrol, Triavil)*. Often causes inability to urinate, dizziness, and drowsiness.

Arthritis Drugs

Indomethacin *(Indocin)*. Causes confusion, headaches.

Phenylbutazone *(Butazolidin)*. Risk of bone marrow toxicity.

Diabetes Drugs

Chlorpropamide *(Diabinese)*. Can cause dangerous fluid retention.

Pain Relievers

Propoxyphene *(Darvon, Darvocet, Wygesic)*. Addictive and little more effective than aspirin.

Pentazocine *(Talwin)*. Addictive.

Dementia Treatments

Cyclandelate Not shown to be effective.

Isoxsuprine Not shown to be effective.

Blood Thinners

Dipyridamole *(Persantine)*. Except for inpatients with artificial heart valves, not shown to be effective.

Muscle Relaxants, Spasm Relievers

Cyclobenzaprine *(Flexeril)*. Can cause dizziness, drowsiness, fainting.

Orphenadrine *(Norflex, Norgesic)*. Can cause dizziness, drowsiness, fainting.

Methocarbamol *(Robaxin)*. May cause dizziness or drowsiness.

Carisoprodol *(Soma)*. Potential for central nervous system toxicity.

Anti-Nausea, Anti-Vomiting Drugs

Trimethobenzamide *(Tigan)*. May cause drowsiness, dizziness, and other reactions.

Anti-Hypertensive Drugs

Propranolol *(Inderal)*. Feeling slowed mentally and physically.

Methyldopa *(Aldoril, Aldomet)*. Feeling slowed mentally and physically.

Reserpine *(Regroton, Hydropres)*. Depression.

From "Inappropriate Drug Prescribing for the Community-Dwelling Elderly" by Sharon M. Wilson, David U. Himmelstein, M.D. and Steffie Woolhandler, M.D. *Journal of the American Medical Association* 272 (1994): 292-296. Reprinted by permission.

- outdated medicines
- inappropriate drug interactions
- patient confusion over drugs with similar names
- over/under-utilization when the patient has not understood the instructions
- pills borrowed from friends
- duplicate prescriptions—from different doctors—with serious potential for overdose.

Questions to Ask About Your Medications

Just as it's important to get thorough medical checkups, it's also important to be informed about your medications. When new medications are prescribed for you, ask your health professional whether the drug has any addiction potential. Inform the physician if you have any history of addiction or if you have any concerns about such drugs. In addition, The National Council on Patient Information and Education recommends you ask the following questions about every drug that is prescribed for you.

1. What is the name of the medicine and what is it for? Is this the brand name or the generic name?
2. Is the generic version of the medication available?
3. How and when do I take it—and for how long?
4. What foods, drinks, other medicines, dietary supplements, or activities should I avoid while taking this medication?
5. When should I expect the medication to begin to work, and how will I know if it is working? Are there any tests required with the medicine (for example, to check liver or kidney function)?

6. Are there any side effects? If so, what are they, and what do I do if they occur?

7. Will this drug work safely with the other prescriptions and nonprescription medications I am taking? Will is work safely with any dietary or herbal supplements I am taking?

8. Can I get a refill? If so, when?

9. How should I store this medication?

10. Is there any written information available about this medication?

Finally, it is helpful for senior citizens to have all medications filled at one pharmacy, where patient medication lists are maintained on a computer; the computer will call attention to any new drug that has the potential to interact negatively with other drugs. It's also important to safeguard against the tendency of seniors to take a drug indefinitely once it has been prescribed. If a medicine review is done every three months, for example, the physician can be asked if a specific drug is still indicated.

We like to think of Grandma and Grandpa as a Norman Rockwell picture, over a turkey at Thanksgiving. But in reality, drug and alcohol addiction is far more common among seniors than most people think.

Carol Colleran
Hanley-Hazelden Foundation

For information on setting up community "Brown Bag Days," write to the National Council on Patient Information and Education (NCPIE), 4915 St. Elmo Avenue, Suite 505, Bethesda, Maryland 20814.

Caution About Over-the-Counter Drugs

While senior citizens take three times the amount of drugs as the rest of the population, their use of over-the-counter medications is even greater. To many, drugs bought over the counter may seem harmless, compared to prescription drugs. However, the active ingredients in pills purchased over the counter can be harmful to seniors. "For example, some of the ingredients in over-the-counter sleep aids are potent and can cause confusion and delirium in senior citizens," according to Myron Weiner, M.D., a geriatric psychiatrist and expert on medications and the elderly. Weiner also warns that herbal potions may cause problems. "People tend to think these herbals are harmless since they're not really drugs, but the ingredients can be potent and cause negative interactions with other drugs. Patients need to check with their pharmacists or doctors to see if there is a danger of adverse interaction with other drugs being taken."

Part II

Obtaining Fraudulent Prescriptions

8

Why Health Professionals Misprescribe

A woman shows up in a doctor's office, saying she's just moved to town. She tells the physician that she has chronic migraine headaches and insists that Vicodin is the only drug that gives her relief. The physician gives the woman the benefit of the doubt and prescribes the drug. She leaves and later uses the drug to alter her mood. She does not have a problem with headaches.

Across town, a young man appears in a hospital emergency room on the weekend, complaining of a severe toothache. He can't see his dentist until Monday and needs a painkiller badly, he tells the ER staff. The man leaves with a prescription for Tylenol with Codeine, a drug he'll use to numb emotional pain.

The scenarios go on and on—problems with migraines, kidney stones, backache. These fraudulent schemes are limited only by the creativity of the drug abuser. These self-medicating drug seekers usually request specific medications and show no interest in confirming a diagnosis or undertaking other forms of treatment.

Addicts often regard health professionals as "easy marks" due to their training, which is geared to helping people and delivering relief from pain.

Health Professionals Are Vulnerable

It's estimated that between 80 and 90 percent of all pharmaceutical drug diversions occur in doctors' offices, at pharmacy counters, and in hospitals. Doctor shoppers, those who go from doctor to doctor, constitute the greatest portion of prescription drug diversion. Typically, these individuals will also use multiple pharmacies. Many of these individuals are acquiring drugs to self-medicate. Others may be reselling the drugs for profit.

The American Medical Association (AMA) has adopted a "4-D physician classification" to explain why physicians, or other health professionals such as physician assistants and advanced nurse practitioners, might misprescribe. The four categories are: duped, dated, dishonest, and disabled.

Duped

Here, the physician is most vulnerable. Failing to detect deception, a physician may be duped into prescribing drugs for a dishonest patient. It is the patient who has failed to meet his or her responsibility in the patient-physician relationship. Doctors are often inclined to trust a patient's description of pain, given that in approximately 60 percent of patient visits to a primary care doctor a physical cause of a patient's symptoms cannot be found.

The scams used by the deceiving patient range from the simple to the elaborate. Given the right circumstances, any physician may be deceived.

Dated

The dated doctor fails to keep current with prescribing practices or knowledge about current drug abuse patterns. A physician might misprescribe psychoactive drugs because the data on which that prescription is based are obsolete.

A number of doctors acknowledge that many medical schools do not adequately teach how to prescribe controlled substances. For years, the view that drug and alcohol abuse were moral problems has resulted in the omission of these subjects from medical school course work. A national survey of medical students found that few have received adequate substance-abuse training:

- No training on addiction—20 percent
- A small amount of training—56 percent
- A moderate amount of training—24 percent

Still, according to statistics from the AMA, addiction disorders affect 20 to 50 percent of hospitalized patients, 15 to 30 percent of patients seen in primary care physicians' offices, and up to 50 percent of patients with psychiatric illnesses. However, many of these cases of addiction go undiagnosed.

Dishonest

According to the AMA, only 1 percent (approximately 5,000 to 7,000) of the nation's doctors fall into the "dishonest" category. These physicians, or so-called script docs, are those who use their medical licenses to deal drugs. Even though only a very small percentage of health professionals are considered dishonest, this group of professionals has been known to illegally prescribe vast quantities of drugs.

A case involving a physician in Illinois demonstrates the damage one dishonest doctor can cause. The physician, along with sixteen other defendants, were arrested for diverting nearly 60,000 tablets of the prescription drug Dilaudid, a painkiller. The street value of the drug was nearly $17 million.

In Indiana, a physician was arrested after prescribing large amounts of Seconal, Percocet, Placidyl, Valium, and Fastin. Investigators estimate that only 5 percent of his practice was legitimate. His small waiting room was typically packed with up to twenty-five people, all waiting for bogus prescriptions. At one point, only two pharmacies were willing to fill the prescriptions he wrote. Both pharmacies were later closed down.

As one California Bureau of Narcotic Enforcement agent explained, "We talk to addicts who are informants, and they tell us which doctors they go to. The informants say, 'All you have to do is give the doctor some phony excuse. He just needs something to write down [as an illness], and he'll charge you $150 for it. You probably spend about five minutes there.'"

Physician and Patient Contribution in the AMA Categories of Misprescribing Physicians

AMA Category	Physician's Contribution	Patient's Contribution
Duped	Fails to detect deception. Allows himself or herself to be manipulated into prescribing at variance with accepted medical practices.	Falsifies or withholds information.
Dated	Fails to keep current with prescribing practices or knowledge about current drug abuse patterns.	. . . .
Dishonest	Subverts medical practice for personal gain.	Uses doctor as a drug dealer, not for medical care.
Disabled	Fails to exercise optimal judgment due to impairment.	. . . .

Disabled (Impaired)

The disabled physician misprescribes because of his or her own impairment, mental illness, or misuse of self-prescribed psychotropic medications. Several studies show that health professionals have a higher prevalence of substance abuse than the general population. This trend is due, in part, to their access to controlled substances. Narcotics rank second among the substances most often misused by health professionals; alcohol ranks first.

Another study estimates that 2 percent of the nation's physicians are chemically impaired each year. The same research points out that 8 percent of physicians are chemically dependent at some point in their lifetimes.

"If you're going to have a medical license, you should be drug tested," insists Robert L. DuPont, M.D. "I don't understand a society that says we will test bus drivers, but we won't test surgeons."

Beyond the 4 Ds

There are, perhaps, "gray areas" in the AMA's 4-D classifications. Some doctors cite the "GOMER" syndrome—the "get out of my emergency room" scenario in which a tired, exasperated doctor may write a prescription in order to be rid of a demanding patient.

Other doctors have described a dilemma that often occurs with patients whose families they've treated for years. One retired physician, an internist in family practice in the Midwest, cites an example of a tough judgment call. "Let's say you get a midnight call from the adult daughter of one of your elderly patients. The daughter is beside herself—her mother is not sleeping, is agitated, and anxious. Do I as the physician take the hard-nosed approach

125

and say tranquilizers may not be appropriate for this elderly patient because the drugs could be abused? Or do I do the compassionate thing and try to help this patient and family who's suffering? If I do, some might call this inappropriate prescribing. But we family physicians know what it's like to get these calls at midnight, on weekends or holidays. These issues are not always black-and-white."

Physician and Patient Responsibilities for Preventing Drug Abuse

Responsibilities of the Physician	**Responsibilities of the Patient**
To have the patient's well-being as the primary concern	To seek medical attention for conditions that he or she believes a physician can cure or ameliorate
To formulate a working diagnosis of the patient's problems based on the patient's history and by examination of the patient	To be truthful in relating historical information and to cooperate with the physical examination
To order appropriate lab tests (or consultations with a specialist) to clarify a diagnosis	To tell physicians about all other physicians providing treatment and about all other medications being taken
To prescribe appropriate therapy (This assumes the physician is acting within his/her scope of expertise.)	To obtain the lab tests or consultations requested by the physician
To monitor the effect of treatment, including the side effects or toxicity of any drugs prescribed	To comply with the physician's instructions (This includes taking medications as prescribed.)
To continue follow-up until the condition is relieved or the patient's care is assumed by another physician	To report symptoms accurately
	To follow through with appointments until discharged by the physician

9

How Drugs Are Diverted from Pharmacies

Three billion prescriptions are filled every year in the United States. That's roughly 8 million a day. These prescriptions are dispensed from the 33,000 pharmacies operated by drugstore chains, supermarkets, and mass merchants. The balance of these prescriptions come from another 20,000 pharmacies that operate independently.

The professionals behind the counters, the pharmacists, are the last barrier between the drug abuser and his or her drug of choice. However, just as the medical professional is susceptible to the doctor shopper, pharmacies are vulnerable to the "pharmacy shopper." A variety of techniques are used to obtain drugs fraudulently from drugstores.

Techniques for Diverting Drugs from Pharmacies

- Forging prescriptions by stealing or photocopying prescription pads and forging the prescribers' signatures
- Counterfeiting prescriptions by making hundreds of copies of legitimate physicians' prescriptions and then forging prescribers' signatures

- Passing fraudulently obtained prescriptions (patient feigned illness or doctor was dishonest)
- Posing as a physician or a member of a physician's office staff, in person or on the telephone
- Theft, robbery, or elaborate scams

In addition to doctor shopping, presenting forged prescriptions to pharmacies is the most common technique used by those obtaining prescriptions fraudulently. Why do individuals take a chance at passing forged prescriptions? The offense is often perceived by offenders as victimless—no one is really getting hurt. The chances of arrest are often minimal, and if apprehended penalties are often minimal. And, the practice can be lucrative if the offender is selling the drugs to others.

Rob's Story

Rob, 34, a businessman from the Midwest, became very adept at diverting controlled substances from pharmacies. He, like many others, believed that health professionals, due to their professionalism and lack of addiction training, could be easily exploited.

I was coming off a year's binge with cocaine. I had gone through several hundred thousand dollars' worth of coke. I lost my house, my friends, my job. I could no longer afford cocaine, so I went back to morphine and Demerol, which I'd been on as a teenager after being seriously injured by a shotgun blast in a hunting accident.

In the beginning of my drug seeking, I went to doctors' offices, feigning back ailments to get prescriptions. But a lot of doctors were suspicious and I didn't get what I wanted. I could get some prescriptions but not for the heavy drugs I wanted or for the quantities I needed. I really wasn't quenching the habit that I had. So I eventually stole a prescription pad from one doctor's office; I had his DEA number, so I just wrote my own prescriptions for what I wanted. Eventually, I stole other pads from other doctors and hospitals. At one time, I had thirty to forty pads from different doctors.

I knew one doctor and one dentist who would give me a prescription, as a kickback, when I made an appointment with them. This, however, was the exception rather than the rule. I think I had hit about every pharmacy in the metropolitan area. I was worried about getting caught. But of all the prescriptions I got filled, I would say I got turned down only about 1 percent of the time. And, I don't think I was that good at what I was doing. I just think some pharmacists didn't know what to do with a suspicious prescription. A few pharmacists just turned their heads. I was very comfortable going to some drugstores. I don't know if they just wanted the business or didn't want the hassle of reporting me. But I would go in their stores, often high on drugs. They had to have noticed.

My drug of choice was Demerol, which is synthetic morphine. On an average day, I was going through 1,500 milligrams of Demerol. The drug came in 50-milligram and 100-milligram tablets. A typical prescription for bad pain might be one 50-milligram tablet every four hours. So, I'd say a high dosage would be 300 milligrams a day. My habit was progressive, getting worse over time.

It was easy to get drugs. I would get one or two prescriptions a day. My preferred method of using was to inject it, so I would dissolve the tablets in saline solution. I'd buy a box of needles and would shoot up maybe ten to twelve times a day. I was going through dozens of needles. The veins in my arms and legs were so collapsed, the only way I could tap into my vascular system was through my jugular vein. I'd sit in front of a mirror and shoot up through my jugular, which had a two-inch by one-quarter-inch scab over it at that point. I would poke through the scab to inject myself. It was hideous, but I could not stop. I was hauled to the hospital by ambulance several times for overdosing. My day-to-day life revolved around getting drugs. It was a miserable existence. I lied, cheated. I needed drugs more than food, companionship, or shelter. I looked like a cadaver. Everyone around me told me how sick I was and how I needed help. Unfortunately, I was the last one to realize it.

Eventually, I was arrested. In hindsight, I believe I wanted to get caught. I was crying out for help. In fact, toward the end of my drug spree, I was using my real name and address when I wrote my own prescriptions.

The day I was arrested, I had gone to the same pharmacy twice in one day to get prescriptions filled. The pharmacist had become suspicious. So, when he gave me the second prescription, he gave me only half the pills, explaining that he was out of them and that I'd have to come back for the second half. I thought it might be a setup, but I was also an addict so I went back later for the second half. I even waited for thirty minutes.

The pharmacist had called the police and they came and arrested me. Initially I was terrified of what was going to happen to me, but at the same time I was relieved that things were coming to an end. On some level I knew I was very sick and needed help. Anyone living the life I was can expect to sit down to a banquet of consequences. I was long overdue.

I faced a five-to-ten year jail term, but I was lucky—I got probation. I'm now in recovery. I speak to recovery groups around town. I think very few people have an understanding of the scope of prescription drug abuse and addiction. My case was extreme, but a lot of others are abusing on a lesser level; they think it's okay because it's a prescription drug.

Risk Factors for Fraud at Pharmacies

Lack of Computer Tracking

Generally, pharmacies do not have computers that are networked outside their own store or chain. This makes it difficult to identify customers who may be obtaining excessive amounts of controlled substances from various area pharmacies. Of course, this is not the case when a customer's prescription is being paid for by an insurance company, which monitors individual prescriptions. Nor would it be the case in a state with a prescription monitoring program. (See chapter 10 on prescription monitoring systems.)

How Insurance Companies Monitor Medications

About 75 percent of all prescriptions are paid for by third-party insurance. When you pay for a prescription with an insurance card, your prescription information is analyzed through the insurance company's computer software. The technology involved is similar to that used to approve credit card purchases. When a pharmacy submits a claim for payment, the insurance company notifies the pharmacy almost instantaneously whether or not the insurance plan will pay for the prescription. And within a matter of seconds the insurance claim will undergo more than 100 different computer checks, called *edits*. The editing process will consider such items as:

- what other drugs the patient may be taking
- the quantity requested
- how recently a prescription for a similar drug was filled

If a patient attempts to overuse a particular drug or class of drugs, the insurance company will send the pharmacy an "alert" that the prescription may not be within the guidelines of the plan. In such cases, the insurance plan will not pay for the prescription and the pharmacist will likely refuse to fill it.

If the pharmacist feels the prescription should be filled, he or she has the option of contacting the insurance company to advocate on behalf of the patient for authorization to fill the prescription. Or, the pharmacist may contact the prescribing health professional and suggest that he or she select a drug that the insurance company would likely cover. Of course, the pharmacist may inform the patient that the insurance company will not cover the prescription, in which case the patient may choose to pay cash for it.

Pharmacists are required to refuse to fill a prescription if they have reason to believe the patient has presented a prescription order that is fraudulent, or if they otherwise feel the prescription is inappropriate for the patient.

When patients are not covered by insurance plans or Medicaid, or prescriptions are denied by such plans, it becomes more difficult for pharmacists to perform their professional and legal responsibilities to curb drug abuse. If they do not know the patient well, they must depend upon their best professional judgment about the patient and the authenticity of the order for the prescription. In such cases, pharmacists will usually contact the prescriber to verify that the prescription is valid and the medication is needed.

Depending on their staffing, pharmacists and technicians may not have the time to investigate all possible bogus prescriptions. If staffing is short, pharmacists may have to consider the degrees of alerts. For example, the alerts that pharmacists pay most attention to are those that deal with a patient receiving a new drug that is not compatible with another drug currently being taken; such medication incompatibilities can be life-threatening.

Pressure to Produce Profits

Some pharmacies may be under pressure to reach financial goals, making it more difficult for pharmacists to take time to investigate suspicious prescriptions. Consider that the average cost of a prescription today is $54, and pharmacies operate on a 2 percent profit margin. Out of every dollar spent for a prescription, 78 cents pays for the manufacture of the drug and another 2 cents goes to wholesalers. Out of the remaining 20 cents, a pharmacy must pay salaries and overhead. Accordingly, some pharmacies are under pressure to sell higher volumes of drugs. Today, an average chain-store pharmacist fills an average of 86 prescriptions a day, compared to 56 in 1993.

According to one pharmacist from the Midwest, "Many of these work scenarios are daunting. I once had a supervisor tell me, 'We pay you to type labels, not visit with customers.' A lot of pharmacists are concerned about this, especially once they have to start doing 200 to 400 scripts a day."

At the same time, while the number of prescriptions being filled has increased dramatically in recent years, the pharmacy industry is dealing with a critical shortage of pharmacists. This insufficient labor pool creates additional pressure on those on the job. And, pharmacists are often overburdened with trying to contact prescribers about prescription discrepancies and processing paperwork related to insurance companies and health plans.

Lack of Familiarity with Customers

In days past, pharmacists in smaller, neighborhood pharmacies were more likely to recognize regular customers. Anyone passing a suspicious prescription was fairly easily detected. Nowadays, larger pharmacies have larger customer bases, making it more difficult for pharmacists to recognize suspicious customers. Larger chain stores may also rotate pharmacists and use "floaters," employees who move from store to store; these employees would not be as familiar with the regular customers, making it more difficult for them to recognize the suspicious customers.

Dishonest or Addicted Pharmacy Employees

As mentioned earlier, about 1 percent of doctors in the nation are considered dishonest and likely to become involved in writing fraudulent prescriptions. Similarly, it's estimated that about 1 percent of pharmacists may be involved in the illegal dispensing of controlled substances. Nowadays, however, more employees have access to pharmacies, increasing the possibility of diversion. These employees include pharmacy clerks and technicians, who may not be subject to background checks, and interns, who are pharmacy students. In many cases, store managers, who are not pharmacists, may also have access to pharmaceuticals.

"Many stores hire high school kids to work as pharmacy clerks, and some of them have opportunities to steal drugs," explains John Mudri, a former DEA diversion investigator who spent thirty years investigating the diversion of pharmaceuticals. Many of his investigations involved drugstores. "I've been told by many store managers that their biggest problem with theft is from store clerks." In one case, a Bradenton, Florida, teenager stole narcotics for two years before finally being arrested. "She would create bogus prescriptions for Vicodin and Lortabs, and have her friends pick them up at the drive-through window."

As a result of such crimes, some chain pharmacies have developed security teams that work to prevent fraud and theft by employees. When employees are caught stealing drugs, they are fired and reported to law enforcement.

Health professionals, including pharmacists, may divert prescription drugs because of personal addiction. Because of their access to drugs, pharmacists may abuse pharmaceuticals rather than alcohol or street drugs.

Reluctance to Report Suspicious Customers

Even when forgeries are spotted, pharmacists may be reluctant to report them to law enforcement. Why? In years past, prior to law enforcement taking a more active role in investigating prescription drug diversion, pharmacists didn't have the support of law enforcement. They didn't know whom to call. In addition, experience has taught some pharmacists that by reporting an abuser they can find themselves wrapped up in weeks, if not months, of legal wrangling.

Gary, a Dallas-area pharmacist and former professor of pharmacy, explains his frustration with the justice system after reporting a man who presented him with a suspicious prescription at a community pharmacy.

Gary's Story

I was working in a pharmacy several years ago when a guy handed me a suspicious script. The guy was wearing black, high-topped boots, blue jeans with a tow-chain for a belt, a black leather jacket, long hair, and a huge mustache.

I phoned the doctor and confirmed that the script was bogus. So I called the police. They were right across the street, so by the time I hung up the phone, the officers were walking in the door. They arrested this man as he stood in front of the pharmacy counter. Then began the games of the legal system.

A few weeks later, I was instructed to appear in court. Failure to appear is a crime itself. So, of course, I showed up in court. I had waited for three to four hours before I was told the case was postponed. So I went home. It was an inconvenience. I'd lost a half-day at work.

Two weeks later, I went back to court. Again, I waited hours. Again, the case was postponed. The attorney for the defendant was hoping that I eventually would not show up, and since I was the witness, the case would be automatically thrown out of court. I was told this tactic is common.

We finally had the hearing about six weeks after the initial arrest. When the defendant came into the courtroom, he'd had a total makeover. He was no longer a motorcycle rogue. He was clean shaven, his hair had been cut, and he wore a suit. The whole crux of the defense was, "Can you recognize him?"

Right or wrong, the issue here was not guilt or innocence, but rather court-room chicanery. This was an example of our legal system being without ethics. There was only one principle: Win any way you can. Freeing guilty individuals often bears no weight on the conscience of the legal system.

In the courtroom that day, there was no question in my mind I was looking at the same guy who'd passed me the forged script. But I'd only seen him for a few minutes six weeks earlier, and I was supposed to swear it was the same guy?

When I was asked by the defendant's attorney if the man in the suit was the guy I saw in the store, I could only say, "I think it is." The attorney harassed me, pointing out twenty guys in the courtroom who had mustaches. How, he asked, did I not know if one of them was the suspect?

Eventually, the guy was convicted. My story is not unique. I hear routinely from other pharmacists that they're tired of similar tactics used by the legal system. I have yet to go to a meeting of pharmacists where I don't hear stories of similar experiences. Consequently, a lot of pharmacists just don't want to report someone because of the abusive nature of the court system. The pharmacists may simply give a suspicious script back to the customer or may tell them they're out of the drug.

Pharmaceutical Companies' Role in Curbing Abuse

Once a drug is shipped from a pharmaceutical company's warehouse, the manufacturer has virtually no control over what happens next to the drug. Yet, the drug companies do have responsibilities for seeing that their products are used appropriately.

Safeguards at the Manufacturing Plant

Drug companies that produce controlled substances take a variety of measures prescribed by state and federal law to prevent diversion. The Controlled Substances Act of 1970 establishes a system of control, from the importation of raw materials for manufacture, through the manufacturing and distribution process, to the dispensing, where the pharmacist hands the drug to a patient.

And companies implement other safeguards. Drugs are kept in vaults in distribution centers, and products are logged in and out. When shipped, the drugs can be transported only by bonded carriers. In many plants, employees are drug tested and are subject to background checks. In some plants, employees are required to wear uniforms without pockets so no pills "sneak" out the door in someone's pocket.

Responsible Sales Representatives

Some advocates of responsible prescription drug use are critical of the fact that a physician's only education about a drug comes from a pharmaceutical rep who works for a for-profit corporation. These critics argue that a sales pitch for a drug does not give physicians enough information about a drug and its addiction potential. The same critics may argue that some sales reps might mislead doctors.

As in any company, there are probably some employees who are less conscientious than others. "Some sales reps may mislead doctors—they may not explain side effects or they may make up answers to questions," explains Tom, a Midwest pharmaceutical rep for twenty-two years. "There is no justification of this, but it happens. Of course, dishonest reps eventually get caught, and this hurts sales as well as the whole industry. Some companies focus on profit while others are more conscientious. Most of us reps know which is which. Most doctors don't."

Another sales rep, David, has been selling pharmaceuticals for fourteen years. He cites a problem in getting access to physicians. "We reps are responsible for informing doctors about products, but sometimes it is difficult getting in to see physicians. They're so busy that they don't always have time to see all the reps. Sometimes, they receive only a brochure we leave behind."

Does Abuse of a Drug Product Hurt Companies?

If a drug becomes highly abused, logic suggests that high-volume sales would increase profits for pharmaceutical companies. However, this point is arguable. Some pharmaceutical company officials say that once a drug becomes known as being highly abused, doctors are reluctant to prescribe it. Sales drop. A case in point is the drug methaqualone, a pain medication also known as "quaaludes," which became highly abused in the 1970s. The drug had a legitimate purpose—the FDA had approved the drug. But the drug was so oversold and abused that it was taken off the market.

Part III

Efforts to Curb Abuse

10

Prescription Drug Monitoring Programs

I f you are a person addicted to prescription drugs, you already know how easy it is to obtain controlled substances from doctors and pharmacies. If you are a relative or a friend of an addicted person, you have no doubt questioned how one person can obtain controlled substances fairly effortlessly. Perhaps you've wondered if your state has some form of computer checks or monitoring to curtail the actions of those who are obtaining drugs fraudulently.

Some state governments are making efforts to curb the abuse of prescription drugs. An increasing number of states have set up *prescription drug monitoring programs* to identify individuals who receive excessive amounts of controlled substances such as narcotic painkillers, tranquilizers, or stimulants. Monitoring programs can help in the following ways:

- Drug abusers are deterred from acquiring drugs to self-medicate.
- Those obtaining fraudulent prescriptions can be confronted and referred to treatment.
- Physicians and pharmacists can help stop abuse by identifying doctor and pharmacy shoppers.

- Law enforcement agencies can detect diversion more quickly.
- States can determine how serious the legal drug problem is and consider education programs, laws, and policies accordingly.

How Do Prescription Drug Monitoring Systems Work?

Basically, once a patient takes a prescription to a pharmacy, the pharmacy sends computerized information to a state agency's confidential prescription database. In most cases, the data is sent by electronic transfer, by computer; in a few states, some information is still sent on paper. Once the data is analyzed, if it appears that an individual may be abusing drugs or that a particular practitioner may be prescribing too many controlled substances, the agency turns the data over to law enforcement. In some cases, those found violating the laws are prosecuted. In other cases, addicted persons are referred to treatment programs.

Monitoring Drugs According to Schedule

States with prescription monitoring programs choose which "schedules" of drugs they will monitor. Controlled substances are ranked by schedules, or categories. The schedule into which a drug is placed depends on these factors:

- known potential for physical or psychological harm
- potential for abuse
- accepted medical use
- accepted safety under medical supervision

How were the rankings established? Recognizing the abuse potential of many medications, Congress enacted the Controlled

Substances Act of 1970 to better regulate the manufacture, distribution, and dispensing of controlled substances. The legislation called for dividing controlled substances into five schedules. For example, Schedule I drugs include such illegal substances as heroin and cocaine. They have a high potential for abuse, but no generally accepted medical use in the United States, and are not available through legal means. Schedules II through V contain drugs with accepted medical uses and abuse potential. Schedule II pharmaceuticals are the most likely to be abused; Schedule V drugs are the least likely to be abused. (See Appendix for a listing of controlled substances by schedule.)

Electronic Data Transfer (EDT)

Under *electronic monitoring* or *electronic data transfer* (*EDT*), after a pharmacist fills a prescription for a controlled substance, the pharmacy sends key information to the state's central database. Typically, the information submitted includes the name of the prescriber and his or her DEA number, the pharmacy's identification number, the patient's name or identification number (often the driver's license number), the National Drug Code (which tells the strength and form of the drug), the quantity dispensed, and date the prescription was filled.

The data is sent to the state for entry into a mainframe computer. Periodic summary reports show the state's prescription activity by categories, including geographic region, physician, pharmacist, patient, and product. Such reports will also identify any of these categories as "outliners," if it appears that any irregular prescribing patterns exist.

With electronic monitoring it is possible to produce a computerized prescription profile for investigation within a few seconds. Before such a program, it may have taken an investigator about eight hours to do a manual search of pharmacy and physician records to create the same profile.

Strengths of Oklahoma's EDT

Oklahoma Schedule Two Abuse Reduction (OSTAR) was the first electronic monitoring program in the nation. It went on-line in January 1991. As the title suggests, under the program only Schedule II drugs are monitored; these include amphetamines, fast-acting barbiturate sedatives, and narcotics, the largest group.

"We've had problems with doctor shoppers who go from doctor to doctor, conning many of them into prescribing large quantities of controlled substances. Then the shoppers would get multiple pharmacies to fill the prescriptions. These problems virtually went away, at least for Schedule II drugs, when we started OSTAR," reports David Hale, Agent in Charge of the Oklahoma Bureau of Narcotics and Dangerous Drugs.

OSTAR also profiles individuals who are arrested while trying to illegally sell or distribute prescription controlled substances. State authorities found that 75 percent of those dealing in illegal sales obtain the prescription drugs through doctor shopping, and/or prescription forgery/counterfeiting. The OSTAR data helps identify these illegal practices, and evidence can be rapidly gathered to prosecute the offenders.

The effectiveness of OSTAR is also demonstrated in the records of drugs purchased from drug dealers by undercover agents of the Oklahoma Bureau of Narcotics and Dangerous Drugs. In the five years before OSTAR, 1986 to 1990, bureau undercover agents purchased 715,055 dosage units of prescription drugs from dealers. But after the implementation of OSTAR, the diversion of prescription drugs into illegal use dropped so rapidly that undercover agents were able to obtain an average of only 281,383 dosage units each year from 1991 to 1996. That is a 61 percent decrease.

OSTAR data also show that the monitoring system has not prompted physicians to change the way they prescribe medications.

Limitations of OSTAR

Although OSTAR has made a dramatic difference in the abuse of Schedule II drugs, it has not had an effect on the diversion of Schedule III and IV pharmaceuticals. Schedule III includes such drugs as Lortabs and Vicodin, which contain the narcotic painkiller hydrocodone. Schedule IV includes benzodiazepines such as Xanax and Valium.

> *OSTAR is so transparent that many physicians are not aware of it. Most doctors haven't changed the way they prescribe, just the few that we identified who were illegally distributing drugs.*
>
> David Hale, Agent
> OSTAR

"We hope that the legislature will change our authority and find the dollars so we can expand OSTAR to cover at least hydrocodone. Right now, we have to depend on manual searches and investigations, which are far too slow and time consuming. We also need to upgrade our ability to create profiles by collecting better identification information," explains Hale.

"It has been frustrating to watch our OSTAR program, the first of its kind, fall behind other states (like Kentucky, Utah, and Nevada) that were able to take EDT and improve it," says Hale. "They are able to track all Schedule II, III, and IV controlled substances, which gives them a considerable advantage over the drug seekers who continue to plague them."

Nevada—Expanding the Reach of Monitoring

The state of Nevada went on-line with its electronic prescription monitoring program on January 1, 1997. The state's Prescription Controlled Substance Abuse Prevention Task Force, with representatives from medical, pharmacy, drug treatment, and law enforcement organizations, drew from Oklahoma's experience with drug monitoring. However, Nevada increased the scope of its monitoring program to include all Schedule II, III, and IV controlled substance prescriptions, not just Schedule II.

The Task Force enhanced the effectiveness of the program by also permitting physicians and pharmacists to obtain "patient profiles" from the prescription monitoring database. This way, doctors and pharmacists could determine what other drugs their patients might be obtaining. This action would help health professionals from becoming victims of doctor shoppers. It would also help doctors and pharmacists refer chemically dependent patients to treatment rather than having them prosecuted and sent to jail.

"The Task Force suspected that there were so many doctor shoppers diverting so many controlled substance prescriptions that law enforcement officers could never investigate fast enough to catch them," according to Keith MacDonald, Executive Director of the Nevada Board of Pharmacy and the individual charged by the Task Force with directing the Nevada EDT program. "Even if the state, counties, and cities hired more police, it would cost too much for investigations, trials, and jails. It was better to let the practitioners and pharmacists deal with as many of the doctor shoppers as they could. This way, law enforcement could focus

States with Prescription Drug Monitoring Programs

State	Program Type	Year Implemented and Schedules Covered	
California	Triplicate/Electronic	1940	Schedule II
Hawaii	Duplicate/Electronic	1943	Schedule II Hydrocodone
Idaho	Duplicate/Electronic	1967	Schedules II, III, IV
Illinois	Triplicate/Electronic*	1961	Schedule II
Indiana	Electronic	1995	Schedules II, III, IV
Kentucky	Electronic	1999	Schedules II, III, IV, V
Massachusetts	Electronic	1992	Schedule II
Michigan	Single Copy/Electronic	1989	Schedule II and Certain Anabolic Steroids
Nevada	Electronic	1997	Schedules II, III, IV
New Mexico	Electronic	1998	Schedule II
New York	Single Copy/Electronic*	1977	Schedule II and Benzodiazepines
Oklahoma	Electronic	1991	Schedule II
Rhode Island	Electronic	1979	Schedules II, III Needles and Syringes
Texas	Triplicate/Electronic*	1982	Schedule II
Utah	Electronic	1996	Schedules II, III, IV, V
Washington	Triplicate*	1987	Selective
West Virginia	Electronic	1996	Schedule II

* Legislation was passed to convert to an electronic program. Washington State operates a limited triplicate program for disciplinary purposes only.

on the really 'bad apples,' those who wouldn't stop when told to do so by their health professionals."

The first major doctor shopper case detected by the Nevada monitoring program involved a man who visited 80 doctors in a twelve-month period; he had 216 prescriptions for controlled substances filled at 84 pharmacies.

Drop in Diversion

Almost immediately, the Nevada program had an effect on doctor shoppers. A review of the statistics bears this out. In the first year, 1997, profiles were developed for 182 individuals, all probable doctor shoppers. Profile results showed each had obtained an average of 159 prescriptions for controlled substances from 22 different physicians and had gotten them filled at 16 different pharmacies.

The Task Force sent the profiles to all the practitioners who had written prescriptions for each of the probable doctor shoppers and to all the pharmacies that had filled the prescriptions. This meant that 1,377 practitioners and 223 pharmacies received one or more profiles. For most of the practitioners and pharmacies, it was the first time they had any idea that other practitioners or pharmacies were involved in treating the same patients. The response was quick. The practitioners reduced the number of prescriptions by 81 percent for the probable doctor shoppers. In the second year, 1998, when Nevada profiled 162 probable doctor shoppers, the effect increased; the practitioners cut back prescriptions for 89 percent of the probable doctor shoppers.

Since then, the Task Force has become even more efficient. In the year 2000, they prepared and sent out profiles on 481 probable doctor shoppers. At the same time, health professionals have taken advantage of the "two-way" reporting system and have increasingly asked for more profiles on patients they suspect of abusing drugs. In the first year, physicians and pharmacists requested 480 profiles. By 2000 they had requested more than 4,500 profiles. In three years' time, the number of drugs dispensed to doctor shoppers decreased 65 percent.

"All this was accomplished with minimum referrals to law enforcement, reports MacDonald. "The program worked as intended. The Task Force only had to involve law enforcement in the most serious cases. The practitioners and pharmacists have been able to intervene with many prescription drug abusers."

Serialized Prescription Monitoring Programs

These systems were formerly called *triplicate programs* or *multiple-copy prescription programs* because they involved triplicate or duplicate copies of prescription forms. Under such plans, the physician kept a copy, and the patient took two copies to the pharmacy, which passed one copy on to a central state agency for data entry into a computer. However, with current technology, states no longer need to receive a paper copy, since data can more easily be transmitted electronically. So most states are changing to single-copy forms with unique serial numbers.

Under the newer *serialized prescription programs*, some of the paper shuffle is reduced with the use of electronics and serialized prescription forms. The state provides the special prescription forms to physicians, dentists, podiatrists, nurse practitioners and veterinarians. These special forms, each of which has a unique serial number, must be used to prescribe certain controlled substances. Once a prescription is written, a patient takes it to a pharmacy, where it is dispensed. The pharmacy then electronically sends the serial number, along with the other prescription information, to the state's confidential central database.

The state tracks incoming data to make sure the prescriptions are written by the practitioners to whom the forms were issued. If forms are lost or stolen, the serial numbers begin showing up in the system and the state can investigate. In the early 1990s a counterfeit ring did attempt to make false serialized forms in New York State. The scheme was quickly identified, five people were arrested, and the operation was shut down.

Success in Curbing Abuse

New York, among the first states to monitor prescription drugs, implemented its monitoring program in 1972. Its serialized prescription monitoring program has demonstrated a dramatic decrease in the abuse of controlled substances, without adversely impacting legitimate prescriptions for controlled substances.

For example, in 1989 New York placed benzodiazepines under the serialized program because they were being heavily abused. In the first year, overdose admissions to hospital emergency rooms involving benzodiazepines declined by 48 percent; nationally, overdose admissions did not decrease. Prescribing for benzodiazepines decreased 44 percent while, in the entire United States, prescribing dropped only 9 percent.

"The Health Department also checked physicians' prescribing patterns to see if there was a change in patients' access to legal controlled substances, including benzodiazepines," explains John L. Eadie, former director of the state's division of public health protection, who oversaw the implementation of the monitoring system. "The department found that 90 percent of the physicians were still prescribing benzodiazepines, with no irregular prescribing patterns. We also found that not all uses of benzodiazepines had gone down. For example, the use of Klonopin (clonazepam) more than doubled after it was placed on the monitoring program."

The monitoring system also eliminated benzodiazepine abuse through the Medicaid system. A group of 3,400 Medicaid patients tracked before 1989 were receiving about 20,000 benzodiazepine prescriptions a month—nearly a quarter million a year! As soon as the monitoring started their monthly use dropped. Within five months, their benzodiazepine prescriptions were down by 95 percent.

Another measure of success was the rapid increase in street prices for diverted benzodiazepines, which increased anywhere from two to five times. Clearly, the price surge shows the monitoring program effectively cut off the supply of diverted drugs.

Pain Management Not Affected by Monitoring

It's important to note that New York's monitoring program does not interfere with legitimate prescribing for severe pain. In fact, morphine prescribing has gone up by more than 1,500 percent since 1980.

Also, through the years, the number of prescriptions for drugs such as Percodan and Dilaudid, narcotics used to treat pain, has been stable. New York has used the program to keep these drugs out of the abuse, so physicians are prescribing them as frequently as when the program started. Clearly, physicians in the state feel free to prescribe these drugs when needed.

Opposition to Serialized Prescription Monitoring Programs

Opposition to such monitoring has traditionally come from the medical community and pharmaceutical manufacturers. DEA officials suggest that manufacturers oppose these programs due to the negative impact on sales. Manufacturers argue that doctors are discouraged from prescribing drugs to patients with legitimate needs for the medication. Many physicians dislike being "watched" by state agencies. Still other critics are concerned that monitoring systems might lead to the inappropriate investigation of legitimate patients.

Early on, New York state also responded to opponents' claims that physicians would avoid monitoring by simply switching patients to drugs not on the serialized prescription program. The department tracked three prescription programs and found that the opponents' claim was untrue. Although a small increase in alternative drug prescribing was noted during the first year, prescribing had dropped back to previous levels by the third year.

Model State Drug Laws

In 1992, the President's Commission on Model State Drug Laws was formed to help states develop laws to fight the drug crisis in America. The Commission, comprised of twenty-four commissioners, included state legislators, treatment service providers, police chiefs, state attorneys general, a housing specialist, district attorneys, a state judge, prevention specialists, attorneys, an urban mayor, and other experts. The work of the Commission was to develop comprehensive model state laws to reduce alcohol and other drug abuse through prevention, education, treatment, enforcement, and corrections.

For six months, Commission task forces held public hearings to gather information on the efforts of successful individuals, programs, and policies. After review and analysis of the testimony, the Commission presented its five-volume final report, which included forty-two model state laws and two policy statements. Issues addressed in their comprehensive report included economic remedies; community mobilization; crimes code enforcement; alcohol and other drug treatment; and drug-free families, schools, and workplaces.

The model laws were first made available in January 1994 for states to consider. States could tailor any portion of the laws to meet their specific needs. The resulting legislation would then be introduced to state legislatures for passage.

Model Prescription Accountability Act

Although the Model State Drug Laws focused on helping states curb the abuse of alcohol and illegal drugs, the problems of prescription drugs did not go unnoticed. "Prescription drug abuse is a very grave problem," states Sherry Green, Executive Director of the National Alliance for Model State Drug Laws. Therefore, the Alliance also drafted the Model Prescription Accountability Act, designed to stop diversion of pharmaceuticals without impeding legitimate prescribing.

At the heart of the Model Prescription Accountability Act was the recommendation for electronic monitoring systems that would collect information on doctors, pharmacists, and patients receiving controlled substances, and compare it with programmed criteria to detect suspicious prescriptions. The act provided a foundation for states to build upon in their efforts to combat prescription drug abuse and its damaging personal and societal effects.

Six-Year Follow-Up Report

In the year 2000, six years after the Commission's inception, members completed a joint study with the DEA on the effects of monitoring programs in those states that had them. Essentially, the study showed that monitoring programs had been successful in curbing abuse, that such programs had not breached the confidentiality of patients, and they had not impeded doctors' prescribing pain medications.

Examples of success:

- In Michigan, officials estimate the monitoring program prevents the diversion of more than 2 million dosage units of controlled substances annually.

- Massachusetts officials report that their electronic monitoring system saves more than 50 percent on their costs of investigating doctor shoppers. It also saves 60 percent on the man-hours worked on such cases. Without the data, a typical doctor shopper case requires 80 man-hours of investigation.

- In Illinois, data collected between 1985 and 1998 clearly show that monitoring had no negative effects on the prescribing patterns of physicians treating patients with legitimate pain. In fact, the number of Schedule II drugs dispensed during the course of the study rose 68 percent.

- In New York, a physician and a pharmacist were arrested after they were detected providing bottles of painkillers and benzodiazepines to a street dealer. The doctor wrote bogus prescriptions, using the names of his elderly patients. The pharmacist filled the prescriptions and passed them on to the dealer.

The Commission's research further shows that monitoring systems have the most benefit when health professionals make effective use of the data available. For example, if a physician accesses the data, he or she may learn for the first time that a patient is doctor-shopping. The physician can then use the data as an intervention tool to guide the patient into treatment. "If done properly, monitoring programs create a number of opportunities to prevent drug abuse, addiction, and the suffering before it happens," Green explains. "So many laws are set up to deal with the aftereffects of a problem, but this is a chance to be proactive."

11

Law Enforcement Efforts

I s doctor shopping against the law? Forging prescriptions? Yes, both are illegal, and in many states are
felonies. Does law enforcement pursue such crimes?
In some cases, yes. In other cases, no.

Historically, law enforcement's attitude about prescription
drug abuse has reflected that of our society as a whole—it's not
been viewed as a serious problem. Accordingly, for decades most
of the training among law enforcement agencies has focused on
illicit drugs. We've all seen it at work—drug busts on the nightly
news, and the resulting community praise. Many police rewards
and promotions are based on the seizure of such illicit drugs as
heroin and cocaine. Indeed, such work deserves praise. However,
the focus on the illegal "drug war" leaves law enforcement
somewhat unprepared for the investigation of pharmaceutical
diversion.

Still, in recent years, some law enforcement agencies have
taken a more active role in the investigation of prescription fraud
and have made strides in combating the problem. But overall, the
nation's law enforcement agencies are underfunded and under-
staffed when it comes to investigating and arresting those involved
in obtaining prescriptions fraudulently.

Local Efforts

Some cities have virtually no resources aimed at investigating prescription fraud; other cities have focused attention on such crimes. Once such city is Cincinnati, Ohio. John Burke formed the police department's pharmaceutical diversion squad there in 1990 and headed the unit for ten years. "That situation is unique. With six investigators, Cincinnati probably has more diversion investigation per capita than any other city," says Burke. "Prescription drug abuse is far more prevalent than most people know, including law enforcement. I guarantee you, these problems exist in every city. In most states, such crimes are felonies. Secondly, they are not victimless crimes. People get high on prescription drugs and commit other crimes such as traffic accidents, burglaries, and thefts."

From 1990 to 1999, the Cincinnati squad averaged 260 felony prescription drug arrests per year. About 40 percent of those apprehended were doctor shoppers; approximately 25 percent were health professionals, of which 70 percent were nurses.

In addition to investigating crime, the Cincinnati squad provides community education. "The team still provides education programs for health professionals to help them spot scammers," explains Burke. "Doctors and pharmacists have known this problem existed for years, but they've not had law enforcement people to turn to in the community. If law enforcement is not working on the problem, whom do the health professionals call? This has been especially true for pharmacists."

State Efforts

At the state level, investigations of drug diversion may be carried out by state law enforcement agencies and/or members of health regulatory boards, including those for pharmacists, nurses, and physicians. Since members of regulatory boards lack the authority to make arrests, they will usually turn matters over to law enforcement agencies after completing an investigation.

Still, most law enforcement agencies have limited funding to hire the investigators and other staff needed to combat the problem. Some states may have only one or two investigators; other states may have considerably more.

Virginia was one of the first states to allocate resources to investigating prescription drug diversion. Virginia also has one of the largest state-level investigative units, with seventeen investigators. The diversion investigative unit investigates two basic categories of individuals. One group includes the doctor shoppers and prescription forgers; these individuals may be acquiring the drugs to self-medicate or sell, or both. The second group includes health professionals—doctors, nurses, and pharmacists—most of whom are self-medicating; however, in some cases, they may be involved in selling drugs illegally.

Investigating Doctor Shoppers

How is a typical doctor-shopping case handled in Virginia? The diversion investigative unit may get a complaint about someone suspected of doctor shopping; the call may come from a doctor, a pharmacist, a family member, or a friend. If an agent is assigned, he or she interviews the doctors and pharmacists involved, and attempts to find out whether the individual is seeing more than one doctor to obtain similar drugs. If the agent determines that one of the doctors would not have prescribed a drug had he or she known the patient was getting the drug from another source, the violation of law is established. A doctor shopper is arrested every 3 days in Virginia.

Investigating the Drug Sellers

"There are certainly more individuals who doctor shop to obtain drugs for themselves than those who acquire the drugs to resell. But we can have more impact if we eliminate a dealer rather than a single doctor shopper," according to Sergeant Rod Bess, Virginia State Police Drug Diversion Unit. A recent investigation involved a ring of scammers in Virginia, Maryland, and Washington, D.C., who were able to divert Dilaudid, a painkiller, by printing their own prescription pads. They used various doctors' names and their DEA numbers when writing the prescriptions. The ring even had bogus phone numbers for doctor's offices—a bank of pay phones they'd set up. Ring members would identify themselves as employees of one of the doctors when a pharmacist would call to verify a prescription. All were eventually arrested.

Investigating Health Professionals

It's believed that the rate of addiction among health professionals may be slightly higher than that of the general population due to their access to controlled substances and the stresses of their work. The statistics on arrests of health professionals in Virginia reflects this belief. From 1989 to 2000, the Virginia drug unit has averaged an arrest of one physician every 44 days, one pharmacist every 48 days, and one nurse every 10 days. In some cases, these health professionals are self-medicating, although some may be involved in for-profit schemes.

"These numbers may be surprising," explains Bess. "However, there is probably an equal number of offenses by health professionals in other states, but the problem may go undetected due to lack of investigative resources."

Community Education

The Virginia diversion investigative unit also provides continuing education to health professionals—hospital employees and administrators, doctors, nurses, and pharmacists. Seminars cover such topics as how to spot scammers, drugs of abuse, and laws against diversion. Between 1996 and 2000, there were 6,759 participants in the unit's education seminars.

Drug Enforcement Administration Efforts

Part of the mandate of the federal government's Drug Enforcement Administration (DEA) is controlling pharmaceutical diversion. The DEA employs approximately 350 field investigators who typically team with other investigators, including those from the FBI, U.S. Customs, FDA, and state and local authorities. The DEA puts its focus on the "bigger players" who may be diverting larger amounts of controlled substances, rather than on the single doctor shopper who acquires drugs for his or her own use.

The DEA estimates that the black market, or illegal diversion of controlled substances, constitutes a multibillion-dollar annual market. For example, an OxyContin tablet prescribed for pain is a sought-after drug on the street. In pharmacies, the drug may cost the consumer $4 per tablet, but on the street it may sell for $10 to $40 or more per tablet. A cancer patient might commonly receive a prescription of 200 to 300 tablets, with a street value upwards of $12,000.

Factors Influencing Prescription Drug Diversion

- *Less risk of disease, especially AIDS.* As addicts look for ways to minimize their risk of HIV infection, more users are turning to prescription drugs because the product is pure, and an oral form can be used rather than an intravenous one. A prime example is the use of Dilaudid instead of injected heroin.
- *Drug abusers are more sophisticated.* They learn how to produce certain psychological effects with combinations of pharmaceuticals which are more predictable in terms of purity, onset, and duration of effect. This means less chance of overdosing.
- *Less risk of detection and arrest.* In some areas, defrauding physicians or pharmacists is only a misdemeanor, in contrast to the felony offense for dealing with illicit drugs. Pharmaceuticals are also often easier to obtain.
- *Financial gain.* Prescription drugs are usually not as expensive as illicit drugs.
- If purchased at retail prices, the sale of pharmaceuticals can be lucrative. For example, the painkiller Dilaudid may cost $2.00 per tablet when purchased in a drug store, but may be sold on the street for $50.00 to $100.00 per tablet.
- *Urine testing by employers.* Often, if a job candidate can demonstrate that he/she is taking a prescription drug and even show the prescription bottle, the candidate is often exempt from negative consequences if a urine test is positive. Sometimes, having a prescription bottle handy will preclude having a urine test altogether.

Retail and Wholesale Level Investigations

Most investigations are aimed at what DEA officials call the "retail level," referring to diversion that takes place in doctors' offices and at pharmacies. The DEA has more than 1 million *registrants*, or individuals who are registered to dispense, administer, or prescribe controlled substances. These registrants include 914, 000 physicians, 60,400 pharmacies, and 60,000 mid-level registrants— mid-wives, physician assistants, and advance nurse practitioners. The majority of the retail-level cases involve "patients" who are obtaining drugs illegally, but in a number of cases also include the health professionals.

> *We do education programs for doctors and pharmacists. Now, they know who to call when they spot a doctor-shopper. In years past, they didn't know who to call.*
>
> John Burke, V.P.
> National Assoc. of Drug
> Diversion Investigators

In a more recent case, DEA agents arrested a physician in Chicago who was obtaining pain relievers and tranquilizers and taking them to Las Vegas, where he sold them, in bags of thirty tablets, in a vitamin store. At the time of his arrest at a Chicago airport, he had 30,000 hydrocodone tablets in his suitcases. Investigators later determined that the doctor had diverted more than 500,000 tablets of hydrocodone and other controlled substances. He was convicted and sentenced to four years in prison.

The DEA also investigates diversion at the wholesale level, which typically would involve large quantities of pharmaceuticals being shipped out of a manufacturer's plant by an unscrupulous employee. DEA officials say this type of diversion is not frequent, but does occur. Investigators make unannounced visits to all manufacturers of controlled substances.

Tactical Diversion Squads

In the late 1990s, the DEA established *tactical diversion squads* to investigate prescription drug diversion. Federally funded, these groups are comprised of DEA investigators and state and local law enforcement officers. The squads are assigned to investigate local diversions. "Some states have dedicated programs to combat drug diversion, and some cities have realized that prescription drug abuse is a serious problem and have set up programs," according to Mike Moy, Chief of Drug Operations Section at the DEA. "In many of these cases, we'll use undercover agents or we'll have an informant we've recruited."

Tracking Shipments of Narcotics

Prescription drug diversion has no geographical boundaries—it occurs throughout the United States. Some of the larger cities have a higher incidence of the crime, but it also occurs in rural areas. To help track the shipping of controlled substances, the DEA uses an automated system known as ARCOS—Automation of Reports and Consolidated Orders System. This system keeps track of where drugs are being shipped. "We can track controlled substances from the point of manufacture to the point of sale, and we often find suspect areas throughout the country," explains Moy.

In recent years, the DEA has also begun making use of prescription data collected by IMS Health, a private company that tracks pharmaceuticals sales and dispensation across the nation. Armed with IMS data, the DEA observes patterns in prescriptions being filled according to zip code.

Drug Courts—An Alternative to Jail

Once law enforcement officers have arrested an individual for a nonviolent crime, related to his or her substance abuse problem, the justice system offers an alternative to jail time. A relatively new phenomenon in the United States, *drug courts* were first started in 1989. Individuals given the option of drug court may have been involved in lower-level crimes such as doctor shopping, driving under the influence, burglary, or loitering. Once in the drug court system, offenders undergo extensive supervision and treatment. "There is constant drug testing, sometimes four to five times a week," explains Susan Weinstein, Chief Counsel for the National Association of Drug Courts. "If you show up 'dirty' in a drug test, there are consequences. If you show up clean, there is a reward. So there is a sanctions and incentives system that you don't usually get in a private treatment plan." The close monitoring also includes regular court appearances.

Drug court involves the full weight of all intervenors—judges, prosecutors, defense counsels, treatment specialists, probation officers, law enforcement, educators, and community leaders—forcing the offender to deal with his or her substance abuse problem. Today, approximately 1,100 drug courts operate across the United States.

Effectiveness of Drug Courts

Studies show that since their inception, 100,000 individuals have participated in drug courts and 71 percent have completed their programs. Studies further show that drug courts are cost effective. Incarcerating an individual costs between $20,000 and $50,000 per year. In contrast, the cost of putting a single offender through a drug court program is $2,500.

12

In Closing

Never doubt the power of small groups to change the world;
indeed, it is the only thing that ever has.
—Margaret Mead, Anthropologist
1901-1978

The country's addiction problems with all substances—alcohol, tobacco, illegal drugs, and legal drugs—represent one of our most serious health hazards. Not only does addiction shred the emotional fabric of our families, but the consequences of untreated substance abuse include traffic accidents and other trauma, poor health, AIDS, dropping out of school, joblessness, underemployment, worker absenteeism, and reduced worker productivity.

More than a half million people die every year because of substance abuse. Drug abuse can reduce life expectancy by about fifteen years. About 50 percent of all preventable deaths are related to some aspect of substance abuse. One out of every five hospital beds is occupied by somebody with substance abuse as a contributing factor.

As a nation, we have taken prescription drug abuse too lightly as a health issue. If the problem is not cocaine or some other street drug, we tend to not think of it as a problem. We need much greater public awareness about this hidden epidemic.

How do we fix this problem? There is no simple answer. The problem is a multifaceted one. But, clearly, education is key. Among the things we can do to combat prescription drug addiction:

- Increase consumer education on addiction and drugs of addiction
- Increase continuing education on addiction for health professionals
- Make addiction treatment programs more accessible
- Promote prevention programs
- Fund law enforcement resources for drug diversion investigation
- Implement treatment programs as part of the justice system for offenders
- Implement prescription monitoring programs

We can readily see that when measures such as treatment and monitoring are taken, positive changes result. We can expand these measures to eliminate suffering and save lives. As a society, we have the intelligence and the ability to make these changes. Now, we must strengthen our resolve to make these changes. Only then can we eliminate more suffering and save more lives.

Appendix

Categories of Controlled Substances

Schedule I

These illegal drugs have no legitimate medical use.
Heroin
LSD
Marijuana
MDA
MDMA (ecstasy)
Methaqualone (quaalude)
Mescaline
Peyote
Phencyclidine (PCP)
Psilocybin

Schedule II

High potential for abuse. Use may lead to severe physical or psychological dependence. Prescriptions must be written in ink or typewritten and signed by the practitioner. Verbal prescriptions must be confirmed in writing within 72 hours and may be given only in a genuine emergency. No refills are permitted.
Alfentanil *(Alfenta)*
Amobarbital *(Amytal)*
Amphetamine *(Dexedrine, Adderall)*
Cocaine
Codeine

Fentanyl *(Sublimaze, Duragesic)*
Glutethimide
Hydromorphone *(Dilaudid)*
Levomethadyl (*ORLAAM*)
Levorphanol *(Levo-Dromoran)*
Meperidine *(Demerol)*
Methadone *(Dolophine)*
Methamphetamine (*Desoxyn*)
Methylphenidate *(Ritalin)*
Morphine (*MS Contin, Oramorph, Roxanol,*
    Duramorph, others)
Opium
Oxycodone *(OxyContin, Percodan, Percocet,*
    Roxicodone, Tylox)
Oxymorphone *(Numorphan)*
Pentobarbital *(Nembutal)*
Phenmetrazine *(Preludin)*
Secobarbital *(Seconal)*
Sufentanil *(Sufenta)*

Schedule III

Potential for abuse. Use may lead to low-to-moderate physical dependence or high psychological dependence. Prescriptions may be oral or written. Up to five refills are permitted within six months.

Anabolic steroids (numerous products such as *Anadrol-50,*
    Deca-Durabolin, Halotestin, Oxandrin, Winstrol)
Benzphetamine *(Didrex)*
Butabarbital *(Butisol)*
Butalbital (*Fiorinal, Fioricet*)

Camphorated tincture of opium (paregoric)
Codeine (low doses combined with non-narcotic medications
    such as *Tylenol, Dronabinol, Marinol, Phenaphen,*
    aspirin, *Empirin, Soma Compound*)
Hydrocodone (with acetaminophen—*Lorcet, Lortab, Vicodin;*
    with aspirin—*Lortab ASA;* with chlorpheniramine—
    Tussionex)
Methyprylon *(Noludar)*
Nalorphine *(Nalline)*
Phendimetrazine *(Plegine)*
Testosterone

Schedule IV

Potential for abuse. Use may lead to physical or psychological dependence. Prescriptions may be oral or written. Up to five refills are permitted within six months.

Alprazolam *(Xanax)*
Butorphanol (*Stadol*)
Chloral Hydrate (*Noctec*)
Chlordiazepoxide *(Librium, Libritabs)*
Clorazepate *(Tranxene)*
Ethchlorvynol *(Placidyl)*
Clonazepam *(KIonopin)*
Diazepam *(Valium)*
Flurazepam *(Dalmane)*
Lorazepam *(Ativan)*
Mephobarbital *(Mebaral)*
Meprobamate *(Equainil, Miltown)*
Midazolam (*Versed*)
Oxazepam *(Serax)*

Pentazocine *(Talwin)*
Pemoline *(Cylert)*
Phentermine *(Fastin)*
Phenobarbital *(Luminal)*
Prazepam *(Centrax)*
Propoxyphene *(Darvon, Darvocet)*
Quazepam *(Doral)*
Temazepam *(Restoril)*
Triazolam *(Halcion)*

Schedule V

Subject to state and local regulation. Abuse potential is low; addictive medication is often combined with non-addicting medicines to reduce abuse potential. A prescription may not be required.

Buprenorphine *(Buprenex, Temgesic)*
Codeine (in low doses combined with non-narcotic
medications such as *Actifed, Novahistine DH, Ambenyl,
Prometh, Phenergan, Dihistine DH, Dimetane-DC,
Robitussin AC, Cheracol)*
Diphenoxylate *(Lomotil)*

For more information on controlled substances, visit the DEA Web site at: www.deadiversion.usdoj.gov/schedules

Resources

Narcotics Anonymous (NA)

World Service Office in Los Angeles
P.O. Box 9999
Van Nuys, CA 91409
(818) 700-9999
www.na.org

Modeled after Alcoholics Anonymous, Narcotics Anonymous is a recovery program offering weekly meetings across the nation. The NA Web site contains information on meeting locations. NA is open to any drug addict, regardless of the particular drug or combination of drugs used, who wishes to become drug free. There are no social, religious, economic, racial, ethnic, national, gender, or class-status membership restrictions. NA membership is completely voluntary.

American Society of Addiction Medicine (ASAM)

4601 North Park Avenue, Arcade Suite 101
Chevy Chase, MD 20815
(301) 656-3920
www.asam.org

ASAM is the nation's medical specialty society dedicated to educating physicians and improving the treatment of individuals suffering from alcoholism and other addictions. The Web site is geared toward health professionals; however, it also contains helpful consumer information, including links to an extensive list of recovery and treatment centers.

Substance Abuse and Mental Health Services Administration (SAMHSA)

5600 Fishers Lane
Rockville, MD 20857
(301) 443-5052
www.samhsa.gov

A federal agency, SAMHSA is charged with improving the quality and availability of prevention, treatment, and rehabilitative services in order to reduce illness, death, disability, and cost to society resulting from substance abuse and mental illnesses. The organization works in partnership with states, communities, and private organizations to address the needs of people with substance abuse and mental illnesses, as well as the community risk factors that contribute to these illnesses.

SAMHSA Substance Abuse Treatment Facility Locator

http://findtreatment.samhsa.gov/

This searchable directory lists locations of facilities around the country that treat alcohol and drug abuse problems. The Locator includes more than 12,000 residential treatment centers, inpatient treatment programs, and outpatient treatment programs for drug abuse and addiction and alcoholism.

National Clearinghouse for Alcohol and Drug Information (NCADI)

www.health.org/newsroom/

A service of SAMHSA, NCADI is the world's largest resource for current information and materials concerning substance abuse. Information and news on both legal and illegal drugs is posted on the Web site.

National Institute on Drug Abuse (NIDA)

6001 Executive Boulevard, Room 5213
Bethesda, MD 20892
(301) 443-1124
www.nida.nih.gov

Part of the National Institutes of Health, NIDA's mission is to bring the power of science to bear on drug abuse and addiction. NIDA supports and conducts research across a broad range of disciplines.

U.S. Pharmacopeia

www.nlm.nih.gov/medlineplus

A service of the National Library of Medicine (NLM), this site provides a Drug Information guide to more than 9,000 prescription and over-the-counter medications. For each drug listed, the site offers brand names, drug descriptions, proper use of medication, precautions while using, and side effects. It also includes updates on warnings and recalls.

Community Anti-Drug Coalitions of America (CADCA)

901 North Pitt Street, Suite 300
Alexandria, VA 22314
1-800-54-CADCA
www.cadca.org

Working with 5,000 community coalition members, CADCA's mission is to create and strengthen the capacity of new and existing coalitions to build safe, healthy, and drug-free communities. The organization supports its members with technical assistance and training, public policy, media strategies and marketing programs, conferences, and special events.

Addiction Resource Guide

P.O. Box 8612
Tarrytown, NY 10591
(914) 725-5151
www.addictionresourceguide.com

A comprehensive on-line directory of addiction treatment facilities, this Web site offers a profile of each of the treatment centers listed. Both inpatient and outpatient treatment centers are listed by both facility name and geographical location.

Nar-Anon Family Group Headquarters

P.O. Box 2562
Palos Verdes Peninsula, CA 90274
www.naranon.com (Pennsylvania site)

Founded in 1967, Nar-Anon is a support group for those who have known feelings of desperation over the abuse of drugs by family members or friends. Although the organization does not currently have a national Web site, visitors are invited to the Pennsylvania site.

Prescription Drug Abuse

www.prescriptionabuse.org

This Web site offers information, news, and research about addiction to prescription drugs. The site posts stories of recovery from addicts and family members; it also features a discussion forum, lists of commonly abused drugs, and an "Ask a Doctor" page.

Prescription Anonymous, Inc.

P.O. Box 1297
Powder Springs, GA 30127-1297
www.prescriptionanonymous.org

A voluntary fellowship of men and women who have taken a pledge of responsibility to carry a message of hope to the millions of people who suffer from prescription drug addiction and/or other mood-altering substances. The Web site offers on-line support and news and information about addiction.

Drug Abuse and Chemical Dependency Resources Guide

http://open-mind.org

This Web site offers one of the most comprehensive lists of drug-abuse-related links available.

Benzodiazepine Anonymous (Los Angeles area)

11633 San Vicente Boulevard, Suite 314
Los Angeles, CA 90049
(310) 652-4100

Formed by individuals in recovery from benzodiazepine addiction, this 12-step group meets weekly in Los Angeles.

American Pain Society

4700 W. Lake Avenue
Glenview, IL 60025
(847) 375-4715
www.ampainsoc.org

Founded in 1977, the American Pain Society is a multidisciplinary organization of basic and clinical scientists, practicing clinicians, policy analysts, and others. The mission of the American Pain Society is to advance pain-related research, education, treatment, and professional practice.

Boston University Medical Center

www.bu.edu/cohis/subsabse/presdrug/presdrug.htm

This Web site contains useful information on commonly abused prescription drugs and illegal drugs.

Alcoholics Anonymous (AA)

475 Riverside Drive
New York, NY 10015
1-800-870-3400 (literature)
1-800-647-1680 (meeting referral)
www.alcoholics-anonymous.org

A recovery program for alcoholics, Alcoholics Anonymous is one of the oldest and most successful self-help programs for recovering from alcoholism.

Adult Children of Alcoholics (ACOA)

P.O. Box 3216
Torrance, CA 90510
(310) 534-1815
www.adultchildren.org

Adult Children of Alcoholics is a program for women and men who grew up in alcoholic or otherwise dysfunctional homes. In meetings across the nation, members gather in a mutually respectful, safe environment to acknowledge common experiences and to discover how their childhood affected them in the past and influences them in the present. Membership is voluntary.

National Association of Addiction Treatment Providers (NAATP)

501 Randolph Drive
Lititz, PA 17543-9049
(717) 581-1901
http://www.naatp.org

The mission of NAATP is to promote, assist, and enhance the delivery of ethical, effective, research-based treatment for alcoholism and other drug addictions.

National Council on Patient Information and Education (NCPIE)
4915 St. Elmo Avenue, Suite 505
Bethesda, MD 20814
(301) 656-8565
www.talkaboutrx.org

Founded in 1982, NCPIE is a nonprofit coalition of nearly 200 organizations, including consumers and other individuals from business, health care, and government agencies. Their mission is to stimulate and improve communication of information on the appropriate use of certain medications by consumers and health care professionals. NCPIE develops programs, provides educational resources, and offers services to advance the common mission of its members.

American Pharmaceutical Association (APhA)
2215 Constitution Avenue NW
Washington, D.C. 20037
(202) 429-7522
www.aphanet.org

APhA is the largest professional association of pharmacists in the United States. The more than 50,000 members of APhA include practicing pharmacists, pharmaceutical scientists, pharmacy students, pharmacy technicians, and others interested in advancing the profession. APhA provides professional information and education for pharmacists and advocates for the improved health of the American public through the provision of comprehensive pharmaceutical care.

National Association of Chain Drug Stores (NACDS)
413 North Lee Street
Alexandria, VA 22313
(703) 549-3001
www.nacds.org

Geared to professionals, NACDS provides a wide range of services to meet the needs of the chain drug industry in accordance with its goals and objectives. The Web site also offers consumer resources, including information about pharmacy care, medicine tips, and links to health, wellness, and substance abuse sites.

National Community Pharmacists Association (NCPA)

205 Daingerfield Road
Alexandria, VA 22314
(703) 683-8200
www.ncpanet.org

The National Community Pharmacists Association, founded in 1898 as the National Association of Retail Druggists (NARD), represents the pharmacist owners, managers, and employees of nearly 25,000 independent community pharmacies across the United States.

Pharmaceutical Research and Manufacturers of America (PhRMA)

1100 15th Street NW
Washington, D.C. 20005
(202) 835-3400
www.phrma.org

PhRMA is the national trade association for more than 100 research-based pharmaceutical companies in the United States. The organization serves as the pharmaceutical industry's voice on policy issues concerning health-care reform, regulation by the FDA, research from the National Institutes of Health, and health-care bills. The Web site also posts news about various prescription drugs and information about new drugs in development.

U.S. Drug Enforcement Administration (DEA)

Diversion Control Program
www.deadiversion.usdoj.gov/

The DEA's Office of Diversion Control is responsible for two distinct problems: the diversion of controlled pharmaceuticals and the diversion of controlled chemicals.

National Association of Drug Diversion Investigators (NADDI)

P.O. Box 42015
Baltimore, MD 21284-2014
(888) 396-2334
www.naddi.org

Established in 1987, NADDI is an organization whose members are responsible for investigating and prosecuting pharmaceutical drug diversion. The organization's objective is to improve the ability of members to investigate and prosecute pharmaceutical drug diversion.

National Association of State Controlled Substance Authorities (NASCSA)

255 Bear Hill Road, 2nd Floor
Waltham, MA 02451
(781) 768-2590
www.nascsa.org
NASCSA promotes communication and cooperation among federal, state and local agencies responsible for regulating appropriate prescription drug activity throughout the various states. The organization also promotes adequate and uniform controlled substance laws throughout the various states.

Index

About the Author

Rod Colvin is the author of *Prescription Drug Abuse —The Hidden Epidemic*. He describes his passion for the topic of prescription drug addiction as coming from the death of his brother Randy, who died as a result of his long-term addiction to prescription drugs.

A former broadcast journalist, Colvin is a producer of documentaries and the author of numerous magazine articles. He is also the author of two other nonfiction books, *Evil Harvest* (Bantam Books, 1992) and *First Heroes* (Irvington Publishers, 1987).

In 1994, Colvin founded Addicus Books, Inc., which publishes a line of consumer health books.

Colvin holds a bachelor of arts degree in sociology from Washburn University and a master of science degree in counseling psychology from Emporia State University.

He can be reached by Email at: RodJColvin@aol.com.

Addicus Books Consumer Health Titles

Cancers of the Mouth and Throat—A Patient's Guide to Treatment   *$14.95*
    1-886039-44-5

Colon & Rectal Cancer—A Patient's Guide to Treatment   *$14.95*
    1-886039-51-8

Coping with Psoriasis—A Patient's Guide to Treatment   *$14.95*
    1-886039-47-X

The Fertility Handbook—A Guide to Getting Pregnant   *$14.95*
    1-886039-55-0 / Nov. 2001

*The Healing Touch—Keeping the Doctor/Patient Relationship
Alive Under Managed Care*   *$9.95*
    1-886039-31-3

LASIK—A Guide to Laser Vision Correction   *$14.95*
    1-886039-54-2

Living with P.C.O.S.—Polycystic Ovarian Syndrome   *$14.95*
    1-886039-49-6

Lung Cancer—A Guide to Treatment & Diagnosis   *$14.95*
    1-886039-43-7

The Macular Degeneration Source Book   *$14.95*
    1-886039-53-4

Overcoming Postpartum Depression and Anxiety   *$12.95*
    1-886930-34-8

Prescription Drug Addiction—The Hidden Epidemic   *$15.95*
    1-886039-52-6

Simple Changes: The Boomer's Guide to a Healthier, Happier Life   *$9.95*
    1-886039-35-6

Straight Talk About Breast Cancer   *$12.95*
    1-886039-21-6

The Stroke Recovery Book   *$14.95*
    1-886039-30-5

The Surgery Handbook—A Guide to Understanding Your Operation   *$14.95*
    1-886039-38-0

Understanding Parkinson's Disease—A Self-Help Guide   *$14.95*
    1-886039-40-2

Please send:

_____copies of_____
                          (*Title of book*)

    at $ _____each   TOTAL   _____

    Nebr. residents add 5% sales tax   _____

    Shipping/Handling
      $4.00 for first book.
      $1.00 for each additional book.   _____

      TOTAL ENCLOSED   _____

Name_____

Address_____

City _____State _____Zip_____
    ☐ Visa   ☐ MasterCard   ☐ Am. Express

Credit card number _____
Expiration date _____

Order by credit card, personal check or money order.

Send to:

Addicus Books
Mail Order Dept.
P.O. Box 45327
Omaha, NE 68145
Or, order TOLL FREE: **800-352-2873**

Or on-line at www.AddicusBooks.com